SCENE:—In the country, near Athens; before the houses of Chremes and Menedemus.

THE SUBJECT

Chremes commands his wife, when pregnant, if she is delivered of a girl immediately to kill the child. Having given birth to a girl, Sostrata delivers her to an old woman named Philtera to be exposed. Instead of doing this, Philtera calls her Antiphila, and brings her up as her own. Clinia, the son of Menedemus, falls in love with her, and treats her as though his wife. Menedemus, on learning this, is very angry, and by his harsh language drives away his son from home. Taking this to heart, and in order to punish himself for his ill-timed severity, Menedemus, though now an aged man, fatigues himself by laboring at agricultural pursuits from morning till night. At the period when the Play commences, Clinia has just returned to Attica, but not daring to go to his father's house, is entertained by Clitipho, the son of Chremes, who is the neighbor of Menedemus. Clitipho then sends for Antiphila, whose supposed mother has recently died, to come and meet her lover. On the same day, Chremes learns from Menedemus how anxious he is for his son's return; and on hearing from his son of the arrival of Clinia, he defers informing Menedemus of it until the next day. Syrus, the servant who has been sent to fetch Antiphila, also brings with him Bacchis, an extravagant Courtesan, the mistress of Clitipho. To conceal the truth from Chremes, they represent to him that Bacchis is the mistress of Clinia, and that Antiphila is one of her maids. Next morning Chremes informs Menedemus of his son's arrival, and of the extravagant conduct of his mistress, but begs that he will conceal from Clinia his knowledge of this fact. Bacchis requiring ten minæ, Syrus devises a plan for obtaining the money from Chremes, while the latter is encouraging him to think of a project against Menedemus. Syrus tells him a story, that the mother of Antiphila had borrowed a thousand drachmæ of Bacchis, and being dead, the girl is left in her hands as a pledge for the money. While these things are going on, Sostrata discovers in Antiphila her own daughter. In order to obtain the money which Bacchis persists in demanding, Syrus suggests to Chremes that it should be represented to Menedemus that Bacchis is the mistress of Clitipho, and that he should be requested to conceal her in his house for a few days; it is also arranged that Clinia shall pretend to his father to be in love with Antiphila, and to beg her as his wife. He is then to ask for money, as though for the wedding, which is to be handed over to Bacchis. Chremes does not at first approve of the plan suggested by Syrus; but he pays down the money for which he has been informed his daughter is a pledge in the hands of Bacchis. This, with his knowledge, is given to Clitipho, who, as Syrus says, is to convey it to Bacchis, who is now in the house of Menedemus, to make the latter more readily believe that she is his mistress. Shortly after this, the plot is discovered by Chremes, who threatens to punish Clitipho and Syrus. The Play concludes with Chremes giving his consent to the marriage of Clinia with Antiphila, and pardoning Clitipho, who promises to abandon the Courtesan, and marry. Unlike the other Plays of Terence and Plautus, the Plot of this Play extends over two days.

THE TITLE OF THE PLAY

It is from the Greek of Menander. Performed at the Megalensian Games; Lucius Cornelius Lentulus and Lucius Valerius Flaccus being Curule Ædiles. Ambivius Turpio performed it. Flaccus, the freedman of Claudius, composed the music. The first time it was performed to the music of treble and bass flutes; the second time, of two treble flutes. It was acted three times; Marcus Juventius and Titus Sempronius being Consuls.[11]

HEAUTONTIMORUMENOS; THE SELF-TORMENTOR

THE SUMMARY OF C. SULPITIUS APOLLINARIS

A severe father compels his son Clinia, in love with Antiphila, to go abroad to the wars; and repenting of what has been done, torments himself in mind. Afterward, when he has returned, unknown to his father, he is entertained at the house of Clitipho. The latter is in love with Bacchis, a Courtesan. When Clinia sends for his much-loved Antiphila, Bacchis comes, as though his mistress, and Antiphila, wearing the garb of her servant; this is done in order that Clitipho may conceal it from his father. He, through the stratagems of Syrus, gets ten minæ from the old man for the Courtesan. Antiphila is discovered to be the sister of Clitipho. Clinia receives her, and Clitipho, another woman, for his wife.

THE PROLOGUE

Lest it should be a matter of surprise to any one of you, why the Poet has assigned to an old man[12] a part that belongs to the young, that I will first explain to you;[13] and then, the reason for my coming I will disclose. An entire Play from an entire Greek one,[14] the Heautontimorumenos, I am to-day about to represent, which from a two-fold plot[15] has been made but one. I have shown that it is new, and what it is: next I would mention who it was that wrote it, and whose in Greek it is, if I did not think that the greater part of you are aware. Now, for what reason I have learned this part, in a few words I will explain. The Poet intended me to be a Pleader,[16] not the Speaker of a Prologue; your decision he asks, and has appointed me the advocate; if this advocate can avail as much by his oral powers as he has excelled in inventing happily, who composed this speech which I am about to recite. For as to malevolent rumors spreading abroad that he has mixed together many Greek Plays while writing a few Latin ones, he does not deny that this is the case, and that he does not repent of so doing; and he affirms that he will do so again. He has the example of good Poets; after which example he thinks it is allowable for him to do what they have done. Then, as to a malevolent old Poet[17] saying that he has suddenly applied himself to dramatic pursuits, relying on the genius of his friends,[18] and not his own natural abilities; on that your judgment, your opinion, will prevail. Wherefore I do entreat you all, that the suggestions of our antagonists may not avail more than those of our favorers. Do you be favorable; grant the means of prospering to those who afford you the means of being spectators of new Plays; those, I mean, without faults: that he may not suppose this said in his behalf who lately made the public give way to a slave as he ran along in the street;[19] why should he take a madman's part? About his faults he will say more when he brings out some other new ones, unless he puts an end to his caviling. Attend with favorable feelings; grant me the opportunity that I may be allowed to act a quiet Play[20] in silence; that the servant everlastingly running about, the angry old man, the gluttonous parasite, the impudent sharper, and the greedy procurer, may not have always to be performed by me with the utmost expense of voice, and the greatest exertion. For my sake come to the conclusion that this request is fair, that so some portion of my labor may be abridged. For nowadays, those who write new Plays do not spare an aged man. If there is any piece requiring exertion, they come running to me; but if it is a light one, it is taken to another Company. In the present one the style is pure. Do you make proof,

Heauton Timorumenos (The Self-Tormentor) by Terence

A Translation by Henry Thomas Riley

Publius Terentius Afer is better known to us as the Roman playwright, Terence.

Much of his life, especially the early part, is either unknown or has conflicting sources and accounts.

His birth date is said to be either 185 BC or a decade earlier: 195 BC. His place of birth is variously listed as in, or, near Carthage, or, in Greek Italy to a woman taken to Carthage as a slave. It is suggested that he lived in the territory of the Libyan tribe that the Romans called Afri, near Carthage, before being brought to Rome as a slave. Probability suggests that it was there, in North Africa, several decades after the destruction of Carthage by the Romans in 146 BC, at the end of the Punic Wars, that Terence spent his early years.

One reliable fact is that he was sold to P. Terentius Lucanus, a Roman senator, who had him educated and, impressed by his literary talents, freed him.

These writing talents were to ensure his legacy as a playwright down through the millennia. His comedies, partially adapted from Greek plays of the late phases of Attic Comedy, were performed for the first time around 170–160 BC. All six of the plays he has known to have written have survived.

Indeed, thanks to his simple conversational Latin, which was both entertaining and direct, Terence's works were heavily used by monasteries and convents during the Middle Ages and The Renaissance. Scribes often learned Latin through the copious copying of Terence's texts. Priests and nuns often learned to speak Latin through re-enactment of Terence's plays. Although his plays often dealt with pagan material, the quality and distinction of his language promoted the copying and preserving of his text by the church. This preservation enabled his work to influence a wide spectrum of later Western drama.

When he was 25 (or 35 depending on which year of birth you ascribe too), Terence travelled to Greece but never returned. It has long been assumed that he died at some point during the journey.

Of his own family nothing is known, except that he fathered a daughter and left a small but valuable estate just outside Rome.

His most famous quotation reads: "Homo sum, humani nihil a me alienum puto", or "I am human, and I think nothing human is alien to me."

Index of Contents

DRAMATIS PERSONÆ
CHREMES,[1] an old gentleman, living in the country.
MENEDEMUS,[2] an old gentleman, his neighbor.
CLINIA,[3] son of Menedemus.
CLITIPHO,[4] son of Chremes.
DROMO,[5] son of Clinia.
SYRUS,[6] servant of Clitipho.
SOSTRATA,[7] wife of Chremes.
ANTIPHILA,[8] a young woman beloved by Clinia.
BACCHIS,[9] a Courtesan, the mistress of Clitipho. The Nurse of Antiphila.
PHRYGIA,[10] maid-servant to Bacchis.

what, in each character,[21] my ability can effect. If I have never greedily set a high price upon my skill, and have come to the conclusion that this is my greatest gain, as far as possible to be subservient to your convenience, establish in me a precedent, that the young may be anxious rather to please you than themselves.

ACT THE FIRST

SCENE I

Enter **CHREMES**, and **MENEDEMUS** with a spade in his hand, who falls to digging.

CHREMES
Although this acquaintanceship between us is of very recent date, from the time in fact of your purchasing an estate here in the neighborhood, yet either your good qualities, or our being neighbors (which I take to be a sort of friendship), induces me to inform you, frankly and familiarly, that you appear to me to labor beyond your years, and beyond what your affairs require. For, in the name of Gods and men, what would you have? What can be your aim? You are, as I conjecture, sixty years of age, or more. No man in these parts has a better or a more valuable estate, no one more servants; and yet you discharge their duties just as diligently as if there were none at all. However early in the morning I go out, and however late in the evening I return home, I see you either digging, or plowing, or doing something, in fact, in the fields. You take respite not an instant, and are quite regardless of yourself. I am very sure that this is not done for your amusement. But really I am vexed how little work is done here.[22] If you were to employ the time you spend in laboring yourself, in keeping your servants at work, you would profit much more.

MENEDEMUS
Have you so much leisure, Chremes, from your own affairs, that you can attend to those of others— those which don't concern you?

CHREMES
I am a man,[23] and nothing that concerns a man do I deem a matter of indifference to me. Suppose that I wish either to advise you in this matter, or to be informed myself: if what you do is right, that I may do the same; if it is not, then that I may dissuade you.

MENEDEMUS
It's requisite for me to do so; do you as it is necessary for you to do.

CHREMES
Is it requisite for any person to torment himself?

MENEDEMUS
It is for me.

CHREMES
If you have any affliction, I could wish it otherwise. But prithee, what sorrow is this of yours? How have you deserved so ill of yourself?

MENEDEMUS
Alas! alas!

[He begins to weep.

CHREMES
Do not weep, but make me acquainted with it, whatever it is. Do not be reserved; fear nothing; trust me, I tell you. Either by consolation, or by counsel, or by any means, I will aid you.

MENEDEMUS
Do you wish to know this matter?

CHREMES
Yes, and for the reason I mentioned to you.

MENEDEMUS
I will tell you.

CHREMES
But still, in the mean time, lay down that rake; don't fatigue yourself.

MENEDEMUS
By no means.

CHREMES
What can be your object?

[Tries to take the rake from him.

MENEDEMUS
Do leave me alone, that I may give myself no respite from my labor.

CHREMES
I will not allow it, I tell you.

[Taking the rake from him.

MENEDEMUS
Ah! that's not fair.

CHREMES [Poising the rake]
Whew! such a heavy one as this, pray!

MENEDEMUS
Such are my deserts.

CHREMES

Now speak.

[Laying down the rake.

MENEDEMUS
I have an only son,—a young man,—alas! why did I say—"I have?"—rather I should say, "I had" one, Chremes:—whether I have him now, or not, is uncertain.

CHREMES
Why so?

MENEDEMUS
You shall know:—There is a poor old woman here, a stranger from Corinth:—her daughter, a young woman, he fell in love with, insomuch that he almost regarded her as his wife; all this took place unknown to me. When I discovered the matter, I began to reprove him, not with gentleness, nor in the way suited to the love-sick mind of a youth, but with violence, and after the usual method of fathers. I was daily reproaching him,—"Look you, do you expect to be allowed any longer to act thus, myself, your father, being alive; to be keeping a mistress pretty much as though your wife? You are mistaken, Clinia, and you don't know me, if you fancy that. I am willing that you should be called my son, just as long as you do what becomes you; but if you do not do so, I shall find out how it becomes me to act toward you. This arises from nothing, in fact, but too much idleness. At your time of life, I did not devote my time to dalliance, but, in consequence of my poverty, departed hence for Asia, and there acquired in arms both riches and military glory." At length the matter came to this,—the youth, from hearing the same things so often, and with such severity, was overcome. He supposed that I, through age and affection, had more judgment and foresight for him than himself. He went off to Asia, Chremes, to serve under the king.

CHREMES
What is it you say?

MENEDEMUS
He departed without my knowledge—and has been gone these three months.

CHREMES
Both are to be blamed—although I still think this step shows an ingenuous and enterprising disposition.

MENEDEMUS
When I learned this from those who were in the secret, I returned home sad, and with feelings almost overwhelmed and distracted through grief. I sit down; my servants run to me; they take off my shoes:[24] then some make all haste to spread the couches,[25] and to prepare a repast; each according to his ability did zealously what he could, in order to alleviate my sorrow. When I observed this, I began to reflect thus:—"What! are so many persons anxious for my sake alone, to pleasure myself only? Are so many female servants to provide me with dress?[26] Shall I alone keep up such an expensive establishment, while my only son, who ought equally, or even more so, to enjoy these things—inasmuch as his age is better suited for the enjoyment of them—him, poor youth, have I driven away from home by my severity! Were I to do this, really I should deem myself deserving of any calamity. But so long as he leads this life of penury, banished from his country through my severity, I will revenge his wrongs upon myself, toiling, making money, saving, and laying up for him." At once I set about it; I left nothing

in the house, neither movables[27] nor clothing; every thing I scraped together. Slaves, male and female, except those who could easily pay for their keep by working in the country, all of them I set up to auction and sold. I at once put up a bill to sell my house.[28] I collected somewhere about fifteen talents, and purchased this farm; here I fatigue myself. I have come to this conclusion, Chremes, that I do my son a less injury, while I am unhappy; and that it is not right for me to enjoy any pleasure here, until such time as he returns home safe to share it with me.

CHREMES
I believe you to be of an affectionate disposition toward your children,[29] and him to be an obedient son, if one were to manage him rightly or prudently. But neither did you understand him sufficiently well, nor he you—a thing that happens where persons don't live on terms of frankness together. You never showed him how highly you valued him, nor did he ever dare put that confidence in you which is due to a father. Had this been done, these troubles would never have befallen you.

MENEDEMUS
Such is the fact, I confess; the greatest fault is on my side.

CHREMES
But still, Menedemus, I hope for the best, and I trust that he'll be here safe before long.

MENEDEMUS
Oh that the Gods would grant it!

CHREMES
They will do so. Now, if it is convenient to you—the festival of Bacchus[30] is being kept here to-day—I wish you to give me your company.

MENEDEMUS
I can not.

CHREMES
Why not? Do, pray, spare yourself a little while. Your absent son would wish you do so.

MENEDEMUS
It is not right that I, who have driven him hence to endure hardships, should now shun them myself.

CHREMES
Is such your determination?

MENEDEMUS
It is.

CHREMES
Then kindly fare you well.

MENEDEMUS
And you the same.

[Goes into his house.

CHREMES, alone.

CHREMES [To himself]
He has forced tears from me, and I do pity him. But as the day is far gone, I must remind Phania, this neighbor of mine, to come to dinner. I'll go see whether he is at home.

[Goes to **PHANIA'S** door, makes the inquiry, and returns.

There was no occasion for me to remind him: they tell me he has been some time already at my house; it's I myself am making my guests wait. I'll go in-doors immediately. But what means the noise at the door of my house? I wonder who's coming out! I'll step aside here.

[He stands aside.

Enter **CLITIPHO**, from the house of **CHREMES**.

CLITIPHO [At the door, to **CLINIA** within]
There is nothing, Clinia, for you to fear as yet: they have not been long by any means: and I am sure that she will be with you presently along with the messenger. Do at once dismiss these causeless apprehensions which are tormenting you.

CHREMES [Apart]
Who is my son talking to?

[Makes his appearance.

CLITIPHO [To himself]
Here comes my father, whom I wished to see: I'll accost him. Father, you have met me opportunely.

CHREMES
What is the matter?

CLITIPHO
Do you know this neighbor of ours, Menedemus?

CHREMES
Very well.

CLITIPHO

Do you know that he has a son?

CHREMES

I have heard that he has; in Asia.

CLITIPHO

He is not in Asia, father; he is at our house.

CHREMES

What is it you say?

CLITIPHO

Upon his arrival, after he had just landed from the ship, I immediately brought him to dine with us; for from our very childhood upward I have always been on intimate terms with him.

CHREMES

You announce to me a great pleasure. How much I wish that Menedemus had accepted my invitation to make one of us: that at my house I might have been the first to surprise him, when not expecting it, with this delight!—and even yet there's time enough—

CLITIPHO

Take care what you do; there is no necessity, father, for doing so.

CHREMES

For what reason?

CLITIPHO

Why, because he is as yet undetermined what to do with himself. He is but just arrived. He fears every thing; his father's displeasure, and how his mistress may be disposed toward him. He loves her to distraction: on her account, this trouble and going abroad took place.

CHREMES

I know it.

CLITIPHO

He has just sent a servant into the city to her, and I ordered our Syrus to go with him.

CHREMES

What does Clinia say?

CLITIPHO

What does he say? That he is wretched.

CHREMES

Wretched? Whom could we less suppose so? What is there wanting for him to enjoy every thing that among men, in fact, are esteemed as blessings? Parents, a country in prosperity, friends, family, relations, riches? And yet, all these are just according to the disposition of him who possesses them. To him who knows how to use them, they are blessings; to him who does not use them rightly, they are evils.

CLITIPHO
Aye, but he always was a morose old man; and now I dread nothing more, father, than that in his displeasure he'll be doing something to him more than is justifiable.

CHREMES
What, he?
[Aside]
But I'll restrain myself; for that the other one should be in fear of his father is of service to him.[31]

CLITIPHO
What is it you are saying to yourself!

CHREMES
I'll tell you. However the case stood, Clinia ought still to have remained at home. Perhaps his father was a little stricter than he liked: he should have put up with it. For whom ought he to bear with, if he would not bear with his own father? Was it reasonable that he should live after his son's humor, or his son after his? And as to charging him with harshness, it is not the fact. For the severities of fathers are generally of one character, those I mean who are in some degree reasonable men.[32] They do not wish their sons to be always wenching; they do not wish them to be always carousing; they give a limited allowance; and yet all this tends to virtuous conduct. But when the mind, Clitipho, has once enslaved itself by vicious appetites, it must of necessity follow similar pursuits. This is a wise maxim, "to take warning from others of what may be to your own advantage."

CLITIPHO
I believe so.

CHREMES
I'll now go hence in-doors, to see what we have for dinner. Do you, seeing what is the time of day, mind and take care not to be any where out of the way.

[Goes into his house, and exit **CLITIPHO**.

ACT THE SECOND

SCENE I

Enter **CLITIPHO**.

CLITIPHO [To himself]
What partial judges are all fathers in regard to all of us young men, in thinking it reasonable for us to become old men all at once from boys, and not to participate in those things which youth is naturally inclined to. They regulate us by their own desires,—such as they now are,—not as they once were. If ever I have a son, he certainly shall find in me an indulgent father. For the means both of knowing and of

pardoning[33] his faults shall be found by me; not like mine, who by means of another person, discloses to me his own sentiments. I'm plagued to death,—when he drinks a little more than usual, what pranks of his own he does relate to me! Now he says, "Take warning from others of what may be to your advantage." How shrewd! He certainly does not know how deaf I am at the moment when he's telling his stories. Just now, the words of my mistress make more impression upon me. "Give me this, and bring me that," she cries; I have nothing to say to her in answer, and no one is there more wretched than myself. But this Clinia, although he, as well, has cares enough of his own, still has a mistress of virtuous and modest breeding, and a stranger to the arts of a courtesan. Mine is a craving, saucy, haughty, extravagant creature, full of lofty airs. Then all that I have to give her is—fair words[34]—for I make it a point not to tell her that I have nothing. This misfortune I met with not long since, nor does my father as yet know any thing of the matter.

[Exit.

SCENE II

Enter **CLINIA** from the house of **CHREMES**.

CLINIA [To himself]
If my love-affairs had been prosperous for me, I am sure she would have been here by this; but I'm afraid that the damsel has been led astray here in my absence. Many things combine to strengthen this opinion in my mind; opportunity, the place, her age, a worthless mother, under whose control she is, with whom nothing but gain is precious.

[Enter **CLITIPHO**.

CLITIPHO
Clinia!

CLINIA
Alas! wretched me!

CLITIPHO
Do, pray, take care that no one coming out of your father's house sees you here by accident.

CLINIA
I will do so; but really my mind presages I know not what misfortune.

CLITIPHO
Do you persist in making up your mind upon that, before you know what is the fact?

CLINIA
Had no misfortune happened, she would have been here by this.

CLITIPHO
She'll be here presently.

CLINIA
When will that presently be?

CLITIPHO
You don't consider that it is a great way from here.[35] Besides, you know the ways of women, while they are bestirring themselves, and while they are making preparations a whole year passes by.

CLINIA
O Clitipho, I'm afraid—

CLITIPHO
Take courage. Look, here comes Dromo, together with Syrus: they are close at hand.

[They stand aside.

SCENE III

Enter **SYRUS** and **DROMO**, conversing at a distance.

SYRUS
Do you say so?

DROMO
'Tis as I told you,—but in the mean time, while we've been carrying on our discourse, these women have been left behind.

CLITIPHO [Apart]
Don't you hear, Clinia? Your mistress is close at hand.

CLINIA [Apart]
Why yes, I do hear now at last, and I see and revive, Clitipho.

DROMO
No wonder; they are so encumbered; they are bringing a troop of female attendants[36] with them.

CLINIA [Apart]
I'm undone! Whence come these female attendants?

CLITIPHO [Apart]
Do you ask me?

SYRUS
We ought not to have left them; what a quantity of things they are bringing!

CLINIA [Apart]

Ah me!

SYRUS
Jewels of gold, and clothes; it's growing late too, and they don't know the way. It was very foolish of us to leave them. Just go back, Dromo, and meet them. Make haste—why do you delay?

[Exit **DROMO**.

CLINIA [Apart]
Woe unto wretched me!—from what high hopes am I fallen!

CLITIPHO [Apart]
What's the matter? Why, what is it that troubles you?

CLINIA [Apart]
Do you ask what it is? Why, don't you see? Attendants, jewels of gold, and clothes, her too, whom I left here with only one little servant girl. Whence do you suppose that they come?

CLITIPHO [Apart]
Oh! now at last I understand you.

SYRUS [To himself]
Good Gods! what a multitude there is! Our house will hardly hold them, I'm sure. How much they will eat! how much they will drink! what will there be more wretched than our old gentleman?

[Catching sight of **CLINIA** and **CLITIPHO**.

But look, I espy the persons I was wanting.

CLINIA [Apart]
Oh Jupiter! Why, where is fidelity gone? While I, distractedly wandering, have abandoned my country for your sake, you, in the mean time, Antiphila, have been enriching yourself, and have forsaken me in these troubles, you for whose sake I am in extreme disgrace, and have been disobedient to my father; on whose account I am now ashamed and grieved, that he who used to lecture me about the manners of these women, advised me in vain, and was not able to wean me away from her:—which, however, I shall now do; whereas when it might have been advantageous to me to do so, I was unwilling. There is no being more wretched than I.

SYRUS [To himself]
He certainly has been misled by our words which we have been speaking here.
[Aloud]
Clinia, you imagine your mistress quite different from what she really is. For both her mode of life is the same, and her disposition toward you is the same as it always was; so far as we could form a judgment from the circumstances themselves.

CLINIA
How so, prithee? For nothing in the world could I rather wish for just now, than that I have suspected this without reason.

SYRUS

This, in the first place, then (that you may not be ignorant of any thing that concerns her); the old woman, who was formerly said to be her mother, was not so.—She is dead: this I overheard by accident from her, as we came along, while she was telling the other one.

CLITIPHO

Pray, who is the other one?

SYRUS

Stay; what I have begun I wish first to relate. Clitipho; I shall come to that afterward.

CLITIPHO

Make haste, then.

SYRUS

First of all, then, when we came to the house, Dromo knocked at the door; a certain old woman came out; when she opened the door, he directly rushed in; I followed; the old woman bolted the door, and returned to her wool. On this occasion might be known, Clinia, or else on none, in what pursuits she passed her life during your absence; when we thus came upon a female unexpectedly. For this circumstance then gave us an opportunity of judging of the course of her daily life; a thing which especially discovers what is the disposition of each individual. We found her industriously plying at the web; plainly clad in a mourning dress,[37] on account of this old woman, I suppose, who was lately dead; without golden ornaments, dressed, besides, just like those who only dress for themselves, and patched up with no worthless woman's trumpery.[38] Her hair was loose, long, and thrown back negligently about her temples.
[To **CLINIA**]
Do you hold your peace.[39]

CLINIA

My dear Syrus, do not without cause throw me into ecstasies, I beseech you.

SYRUS

The old woman was spinning the woof:[40] there was one little servant girl besides;—she was weaving[41] together with them, covered with patched clothes, slovenly, and dirty with filthiness.

CLITIPHO

If this is true, Clinia, as I believe it is, who is there more fortunate than you? Do you mark this girl whom he speaks of, as dirty and drabbish? This, too, is a strong indication that the mistress is out of harm's way, when her confidant is in such ill plight; for it is a rule with those who wish to gain access to the mistress, first to bribe the maid.

CLINIA [To **SYRUS**]

Go on, I beseech you; and beware of endeavoring to purchase favor by telling an untruth. What did she say, when you mentioned me?

SYRUS

When we told her that you had returned, and had requested her to come to you, the damsel instantly put away the web, and covered her face all over with tears; so that you might easily perceive that it really was caused by her affection for you.

CLINIA
So may the Deities bless me, I know not where I am for joy! I was so alarmed before.

CLITIPHO
But I was sure that there was no reason, Clinia. Come now, Syrus, tell me, in my turn, who this other lady is.

SYRUS
Your Bacchis, whom we are bringing.[42]

CLITIPHO
Ha! What! Bacchis? How now, you rascal! whither are you bringing her?

SYRUS
Whither am I bringing her? To our house, to be sure.

CLITIPHO
What! to my father's?

SYRUS
To the very same.

CLITIPHO
Oh, the audacious impudence of the fellow!

SYRUS
Hark'ye, no great and memorable action is done without some risk.

CLITIPHO
Look now; are you seeking to gain credit for yourself, at the hazard of my character, you rascal, in a point, where, if you only make the slightest slip, I am ruined? What would you be doing with her?

SYRUS
But still—

CLITIPHO
Why "still?"

SYRUS
If you'll give me leave, I'll tell you.

CLINIA
Do give him leave.

CLITIPHO

I give him leave then.

SYRUS

This affair is now just as though when—

CLITIPHO

Plague on it, what roundabout story is he beginning to tell me?

CLINIA

Syrus, he says what's right—do omit digressions; come to the point.

SYRUS

Really I can not hold my tongue. Clitipho, you are every way unjust, and can not possibly be endured.

CLINIA

Upon my faith, he ought to have a hearing.
[To **CLITIPHO**]
Do be silent.

SYRUS

You wish to indulge in your amours; you wish to possess your mistress; you wish that to be procured wherewithal to make her presents; in getting this, you do not wish the risk to be your own. You are not wise to no purpose,—if indeed it is being wise to wish for that which can not happen. Either the one must be had with the other, or the one must be let alone with the other. Now, of these two alternatives, consider which one you would prefer; although this project which I have formed, I know to be both a wise and a safe one. For there is an opportunity for your mistress to be with you at your father's house, without fear of a discovery; besides, by these self-same means, I shall find the money which you have promised her—to effect which, you have already made my ears deaf with entreating me. What would you have more?

CLITIPHO

If, indeed, this could be brought about—

SYRUS

If, indeed? You shall know it by experience.

CLITIPHO

Well, well, disclose this project of yours. What is it?

SYRUS [Pointing to **CLINIA**]

We will pretend that your mistress is his.

CLITIPHO

Very fine! Tell me, what is he to do with his own? Is she, too, to be called his, as if one was not a sufficient discredit?

SYRUS

No—she shall be taken to your mother.

CLITIPHO
Why there?

SYRUS
It would be tedious, Clitipho, if I were to tell you why I do so; I have a good reason.

CLITIPHO
Stuff! I see no grounds sufficiently solid why it should be for my advantage to incur this risk.[43]

[Turning as if going.

SYRUS
Stay; if there is this risk, I have another project, which you must both confess to be free from danger.

CLITIPHO
Find out something of that description, I beseech you.

SYRUS
By all means; I'll go meet her, and tell her to return home.

CLITIPHO
Ha! what was it you said?

SYRUS
I'll rid you at once of all fears, so that you may sleep at your ease upon either ear.[44]

CLITIPHO
What am I to do now?

CLINIA
What are you to do? The goods that—

CLITIPHO
Only tell me the truth, Syrus.

SYRUS
Dispatch quickly; you'll be wishing just now too late and in vain.

[Going.

CLINIA
The Gods provide, enjoy while yet you may; for you know not—

CLITIPHO [Calling]
Syrus, I say!

SYRUS [Moving on]
Go on; I shall still do that which I said.[45]

CLINIA
Whether you may have another opportunity hereafter or ever again.

CLITIPHO
I'faith, that's true.
[Calling]
Syrus, Syrus, I say, harkye, harkye, Syrus!

SYRUS [Aside]
He warms a little.
[To **CLITIPHO**]
What is it you want?

CLITIPHO
Come back, come back.

SYRUS [Coming back to him]
Here I am; tell me what you would have. You'll be presently saying that this, too, doesn't please you.

CLITIPHO
Nay, Syrus, I commit myself, and my love, and my reputation entirely to you: you are the seducer; take care you don't deserve any blame.

SYRUS
It is ridiculous for you to give me that caution, Clitipho, as if my interest was less at stake in this affair than yours. Here, if any ill luck should perchance befall us, words will be in readiness for you, but for this individual blows—
[Pointing to himself]
For that reason, this matter is by no means to be neglected on my part: but do prevail upon him—
[Pointing to **CLINIA**]
—to pretend that she is his own mistress.

CLINIA
You may rest assured I'll do so. The matter has now come to that pass, that it is a case of necessity.

CLITIPHO
'Tis with good reason that I love you, Clinia.

CLINIA
But she mustn't be tripping at all.

SYRUS
She is thoroughly tutored in her part.

CLITIPHO

But this I wonder at, how you could so easily prevail upon her, who is wont to treat such great people[46] with scorn.

SYRUS
I came to her at the proper moment, which in all things is of the first importance: for there I found a certain wretched captain soliciting her favors: she artfully managed the man, so as to inflame his eager passions by denial; and this, too, that it might be especially pleasing to yourself. But hark you, take care, will you, not to be imprudently impetuous. You know your father, how quick-sighted he is in these matters; and I know you, how unable you are to command yourself. Keep clear of words of double meaning,[47] your sidelong looks, sighing, hemming, coughing, tittering.

CLITIPHO
You shall have to commend me.

SYRUS
Take care of that, please.

CLITIPHO
You yourself shall be surprised at me.

SYRUS
But how quickly the ladies have come up with us!

CLITIPHO
Where are they?

[**SYRUS** stands before him.

Why do you hold me back?

SYRUS
For the present she is nothing to you.

CLITIPHO
I know it, before my father; but now in the mean time—

SYRUS
Not a bit the more.

CLITIPHO
Do let me.

SYRUS
I will not let you, I tell you.

CLITIPHO
But only for a moment, pray.

SYRUS
I forbid it.

CLITIPHO
Only to salute her.

SYRUS
If you are wise, get you gone.

CLITIPHO
I'm off. But what's he to do?

[Pointing at **CLINIA**.

SYRUS
He will stay here.

CLITIPHO
O happy man!

SYRUS
Take yourself off.

[Exit **CLITIPHO**.

SCENE IV

Enter **BACCHIS** and **ANTIPHILA** at a distance.

BACCHIS
Upon my word, my dear Antiphila, I commend you, and think you fortunate in having made it your study that your manners should be conformable to those good looks of yours: and so may the Gods bless me, I do not at all wonder if every man is in love with you. For your discourse has been a proof to me what kind of disposition you possess. And when now I reflect in my mind upon your way of life, and that of all of you, in fact, who keep the public at a distance from yourselves, it is not surprising both that you are of that disposition, and that we are not; for it is your interest to be virtuous; those, with whom we are acquainted, will not allow us to be so. For our lovers, allured merely by our beauty, court us for that; when that has faded, they transfer their affections elsewhere; and unless we have made provision in the mean time for the future, we live in destitution. Now with you, when you have once resolved to pass your life with one man whose manners are especially kindred to your own, those persons[48] become attached to you. By this kindly feeling, you are truly devoted to each other; and no calamity can ever possibly interrupt your love.

ANTIPHILA
I know nothing about other women: I'm sure that I have, indeed, always used every endeavor to derive my own happiness from his happiness.

CLINIA [Apart, overhearing **ANTIPHILA**]

Ah! 'tis for that reason, my Antiphila, that you alone have now caused me to return to my native country; for while I was absent from you, all other hardships which I encountered were light to me, save the being deprived of you.

SYRUS [Apart]

I believe it.

CLINIA [Apart]

Syrus, I can scarce endure it![49] Wretch that I am, that I should not be allowed to possess one of such a disposition at my own discretion!

SYRUS

Nay, so far as I understand your father, he will for a long time yet be giving you a hard task.

BACCHIS

Why, who is that young man that's looking at us?

ANTIPHILA [Seeing **CLINIA**]

Ah! do support me, I entreat you!

BACCHIS

Prithee, what is the matter with you?

ANTIPHILA

I shall die, alas! I shall die!

BACCHIS

Why are you thus surprised, Antiphila?

ANTIPHILA

Is it Clinia that I see, or not?

BACCHIS

Whom do you see?

CLINIA [Running to embrace **ANTIPHILA**]

Blessings on you, my life!

ANTIPHILA

Oh my long-wished for Clinia, blessings on you!

CLINIA

How fare you, my love?

ANTIPHILA

I'm overjoyed that you have returned safe.

CLINIA
And do I embrace you, Antiphila, so passionately longed for by my soul?

SYRUS
Go in-doors; for the old gentleman has been waiting for us some time.

[They go into the house of **CHREMES**.

SCENE I

Enter **CHREMES** from his house.

CHREMES [To himself]
It is now daybreak.[50] Why do I delay to knock at my neighbor's door, that he may learn from me the first that his son has returned? Although I am aware that the youth would not prefer this. But when I see him tormenting himself so miserably about his absence, can I conceal a joy so unhoped for, especially when there can be no danger to him from the discovery? I will not do so; but as far as I can I will assist the old man. As I see my son aiding his friend and year's-mate, and acting as his confidant in his concerns, it is but right that we old men as well should assist each other.

[Enter **MENEDEMUS** from his house.

MENEDEMUS [To himself]
Assuredly I was either born with a disposition peculiarly suited for misery, or else that saying which I hear commonly repeated, that "time assuages human sorrow," is false. For really my sorrow about my son increases daily; and the longer he is away from me, the more anxiously do I wish for him, and the more I miss him.

CHREMES [Apart]
But I see him coming out of his house; I'll go speak to him.
[Aloud]
Menedemus, good-morrow; I bring you news, which you would especially desire to be imparted.

MENEDEMUS
Pray, have you heard any thing about my son, Chremes?

CHREMES
He's alive, and well.

MENEDEMUS
Why, where is he, pray?

CHREMES

Here, at my house, at home.

MENEDEMUS
My son?

CHREMES
Such is the fact.

MENEDEMUS
Come home?

CHREMES
Certainly.

MENEDEMUS
My son, Clinia, come home?

CHREMES
I say so.

MENEDEMUS
Let us go. Lead me to him, I beg of you.

CHREMES
He does not wish you yet to know of his return, and he shuns your presence; he's afraid that, on account of that fault, your former severity may even be increased.

MENEDEMUS
Did you not tell him how I was affected?[51]

CHREMES
No—

MENEDEMUS
For what reason, Chremes?

CHREMES
Because there you would judge extremely ill both for yourself and for him, if you were to show yourself of a spirit so weak and irresolute.

MENEDEMUS
I can not help it: enough already, enough, have I proved a rigorous father.

CHREMES
Ah Menedemus! you are too precipitate in either extreme, either with profuseness or with parsimony too great. Into the same error will you fall from the one side as from the other. In the first place, formerly, rather than allow your son to visit a young woman, who was then content with a very little, and to whom any thing was acceptable, you frightened him away from here. After that, she began, quite

against her inclination, to seek a subsistence upon the town. Now, when she can not be supported without a great expense, you are ready to give any thing. For, that you may know how perfectly she is trained to extravagance, in the first place, she has already brought with her more than ten female attendants, all laden with clothes and jewels of gold; if a satrap[52] had been her admirer, he never could support her expenses, much less can you.

MENEDEMUS
Is she at your house?

CHREMES
Is she, do you ask? I have felt it; for I have given her and her retinue one dinner; had I to give them another such, it would be all over with me; for, to pass by other matters, what a quantity of wine she did consume for me in tasting only,[53] saying thus, "This wine is too acid,[54] respected sir,[55] do please look for something more mellow." I opened all the casks, all the vessels;[56] she kept all on the stir: and this but a single night. What do you suppose will become of you when they are constantly preying upon you? So may the Gods prosper me, Menedemus, I do pity your lot.

MENEDEMUS
Let him do what he will; let him take, waste, and squander; I'm determined to endure it, so long as I only have him with me.

CHREMES
If it is your determination thus to act, I hold it to be of very great moment that he should not be aware that with a full knowledge you grant him this.

MENEDEMUS
What shall I do?

CHREMES
Any thing, rather than what you are thinking of; supply him with money through some other person; suffer yourself to be imposed upon by the artifices of his servant: although I have smelt out this too, that they are about that, and are secretly planning it among them. Syrus is always whispering with that servant of yours;[57] they impart their plans to the young men; and it were better for you to lose a talent this way, than a mina the other. The money is not the question now, but this—in what way we can supply it to the young man with the least danger. For if he once knows the state of your feelings, that you would sooner part with your life, and sooner with all your money, than allow your son to leave you; whew! what an inlet[58] will you be opening for his debauchery! aye, and so much so, that henceforth to live can not be desirable to you. For we all become worse through indulgence. Whatever comes into his head, he'll be wishing for; nor will he reflect whether that which he desires is right or wrong. You will not be able to endure your estate and him going to ruin. You will refuse to supply him: he will immediately have recourse to the means by which he finds that he has the greatest hold upon you, and threaten that he will immediately leave you.

MENEDEMUS
You seem to speak the truth, and just what is the fact.

CHREMES

I'faith, I have not been sensible of sleep this night with my eyes,[59] for thinking of this—how to restore your son to you.

MENEDEMUS [Taking his hand]
Give me your right hand. I request that you will still act in a like manner, Chremes.

CHREMES
I am ready to serve you.

MENEDEMUS
Do you know what it is I now want you to do?

CHREMES
Tell me.

MENEDEMUS
As you have perceived that they are laying a plan to deceive me, that they may hasten to complete it. I long to give him whatever he wants: I am now longing to behold him.

CHREMES
I'll lend my endeavors. This little business is in my way. Our neighbors Simus and Crito are disputing here about boundaries; they have chosen me for arbitrator. I'll go and tell them that I can not possibly give them my attention to-day as I had stated I would. I'll be here immediately.

[Exit.

MENEDEMUS
Pray do.
[To himself]
Ye Gods, by our trust in you! That the nature of all men should be so constituted, that they can see and judge of other men's affairs better than their own! Is it because in our own concerns we are biased either with joy or grief in too great a degree? How much wiser now is he for me, than I have been for myself!

[Re-enter **CHREMES**.

CHREMES
I have disengaged myself, that I might lend you my services at my leisure. Syrus must be found and instructed by me in this business. Some one, I know not who, is coming out of my house: do you step hence home, that they may not perceive[60] that we are conferring together.

[**MENEDEMUS** goes into his house.

SCENE II

Enter **SYRUS** from the house of **CHREMES**.

SYRUS [Aloud to himself]
Run to and fro in every direction; still, money, you must be found: a trap must be laid for the old man.

CHREMES [Apart, overhearing him]
Was I deceived in saying that they were planning this? That servant of Clinia's is somewhat dull; therefore that province has been assigned to this one of ours.

SYRUS [In a low voice]
Who's that speaking?
[Catches sight of **CHREMES**]
I'm undone! Did he hear it, I wonder?

CHREMES
Syrus.

SYRUS
Well—

CHREMES
What are you doing here?

SYRUS
All right. Really, I am quite surprised at you, Chremes, up so early, after drinking so much yesterday.

CHREMES
Not too much.

SYRUS
Not too much, say you? Really, you've seen the old age of an eagle,[61] as the saying is.

CHREMES
Pooh, pooh!

SYRUS
A pleasant and agreeable woman this Courtesan.

CHREMES
Why, so she seemed to me, in fact.

SYRUS
And really of handsome appearance.

CHREMES
Well enough.

SYRUS

Not like those of former days,[62] but as times are now, very passable: nor do I in the least wonder that Clinia doats upon her. But he has a father—a certain covetous, miserable, and niggardly person—this neighbor of ours.
[Pointing to the house]
Do you know him? Yet, as if he was not abounding in wealth, his son ran away through want. Are you aware that it is the fact, as I am saying?

CHREMES
How should I not be aware? A fellow that deserves the mill.

SYRUS
Who?

CHREMES
That servant of the young gentleman, I mean.

SYRUS [Aside]
Syrus! I was sadly afraid for you.

CHREMES
To suffer it to come to this!

SYRUS
What was he to do?

CHREMES
Do you ask the question? He ought to have found some expedient, contrived some stratagem, by means of which there might have been something for the young man to give to his mistress, and thus have saved this crabbed old fellow in spite of himself.

SYRUS
You are surely joking.

CHREMES
This ought to have been done by him, Syrus.

SYRUS
How now—pray, do you commend servants, who deceive their masters?

CHREMES
Upon occasion—I certainly do commend them.

SYRUS
Quite right.

CHREMES
Inasmuch as it often is the remedy for great disturbances. Then would this man's only son have staid at home.

SYRUS [Aside]
Whether he says this in jest or in earnest, I don't know; only, in fact, that he gives me additional zest for longing still more to trick him.

CHREMES
And what is he now waiting for, Syrus? Is it until his father drives him away from here a second time, when he can no longer support her expenses?[63] Has he no plot on foot against the old gentleman?

SYRUS
He is a stupid fellow.

CHREMES
Then you ought to assist him—for the sake of the young man.

SYRUS
For my part, I can do so easily, if you command me; for I know well in what fashion it is usually done.

CHREMES
So much the better, i' faith.

SYRUS
'Tis not my way to tell an untruth.

CHREMES
Do it then.

SYRUS
But hark you! Just take care and remember this, in case any thing of this sort should perchance happen at a future time, such are human affairs!—your son might do the same.

CHREMES
The necessity will not arise, I trust.

SYRUS
I' faith, and I trust so too: nor do I say so now, because I have suspected him in any way; but in case, none the more[64]—You see what his age is;
[Aside]
—and truly, Chremes,[65] if an occasion does happen, I may be able to handle you right handsomely.

CHREMES
As to that, we'll consider what is requisite when the occasion does happen. At present do you set about this matter.

[Goes into his house.

SYRUS [To himself]

Never on any occasion did I hear my master talk more to the purpose; nor at any time could I believe that I was authorized to play the rogue with greater impunity. I wonder who it is coming out of our house?

[Stands aside.

SCENE III

Enter **CHREMES** and **CLITIPHO** from the house of the former.

CHREMES
Pray, what does this mean? What behavior is this, Clitipho? Is this acting as becomes you?

CLITIPHO
What have I done?

CHREMES
Did I not see you just now putting your hand into this Courtesan's bosom?

SYRUS [Apart]
It's all up with us—I'm utterly undone!

CLITIPHO
What, I?

CHREMES
With these self-same eyes I saw it—don't deny it. Besides, you wrong him unworthily in not keeping your hands off: for indeed it is a gross affront to entertain a person, your friend, at your house, and to take liberties with his mistress. Yesterday, for instance, at wine, how rude you were—

SYRUS [Apart]
'Tis the truth.[66]

CHREMES
How annoying you were! So much so, that for my part, as the Gods may prosper me, I dreaded what in the end might be the consequence. I understand lovers. They resent highly things that you would not imagine.

CLITIPHO
But he has full confidence in me, father, that I would not do any thing of that kind.

CHREMES
Be it so; still, at least, you ought to go somewhere for a little time away from their presence. Passion prompts to many a thing; your presence acts as a restraint upon doing them. I form a judgment from myself. There's not one of my friends this day to whom I would venture, Clitipho, to disclose all my secrets. With one, his station forbids it; with another, I am ashamed of the action itself, lest I may

appear a fool or devoid of shame; do you rest assured that he does the same.[67] But it is our part to be sensible of this; and, when and where it is requisite, to show due complaisance.

SYRUS [Coming forward and whispering to **CLITIPHO**]
What is it he is saying?

CLITIPHO [Aside, to **SYRUS**]
I'm utterly undone!

SYRUS
Clitipho, these same injunctions I gave you. You have acted the part of a prudent and discreet person.[68]

CLITIPHO
Hold your tongue, I beg.

SYRUS
Very good.

CHREMES [Approaching them]
Syrus, I am ashamed of him.

SYRUS
I believe it; and not without reason. Why, he vexes myself even.

CLITIPHO [To **SYRUS**]
Do you persist, then?

SYRUS
I' faith, I'm saying the truth, as it appears to me.

CLITIPHO
May I not go near them?

CHREMES
How now—pray, is there but one way[69] of going near them?

SYRUS [Aside]
Confusion! He'll be betraying himself before I've got the money.
[Aloud]
Chremes, will you give attention to me, who am but a silly person?

CHREMES
What am I to do?

SYRUS
Bid him go somewhere out of the way.

CLITIPHO
Where am I to go?

SYRUS
Where you please; leave the place to them; be off and take a walk.

CLITIPHO
Take a walk! where?

SYRUS
Pshaw! Just as if there was no place to walk in. Why, then, go this way, that way, where you will.

CHREMES
He says right, I'm of his opinion.

CLITIPHO
May the Gods extirpate you, Syrus, for thrusting me away from here.

SYRUS [Aside to **CLITIPHO**]
Then do you for the future keep those hands of yours within bounds.

[Exit **CLITIPHO**.

Really now
[To **CHREMES**]
—what do you think? What do you imagine will become of him next, unless, so far as the Gods afford you the means, you watch him, correct and admonish him?

CHREMES
I'll take care of that.

SYRUS
But now, master, he must be looked after by you.

CHREMES
It shall be done.

SYRUS
If you are wise,—for now he minds me less and less every day.

CHREMES
What say you? What have you done, Syrus, about that matter which I was mentioning to you a short time since? Have you any plan that suits you, or not yet even?

SYRUS
You mean the design upon Menedemus? I have; I have just hit upon one.

CHREMES

You are a clever fellow; what is it? Tell me.

SYRUS
I'll tell you; but, as one matter arises, out of another—

CHREMES
Why, what is it, Syrus?

SYRUS
This Courtesan is a very bad woman.

CHREMES
So she seems.

SYRUS
Aye, if you did but know. O shocking! just see what she is hatching. There was a certain old woman here from Corinth,—this Bacchis lent her a thousand silver drachmæ.

CHREMES
What then?

SYRUS
She is now dead: she has left a daughter, a young girl. She has been left with this Bacchis as a pledge for that sum.

CHREMES
I understand you.

SYRUS
She has brought her hither along with her, her I mean who is now with your wife.[70]

CHREMES
What then?

SYRUS
She is soliciting Clinia at once to advance her this money; she says, however, that this girl is to be a security, that, at a future time, she will repay the thousand pieces of money.

CHREMES
And would she really be a security?[71]

SYRUS
Dear me, is it to be doubted? I think so.

CHREMES
What then do you intend doing?

SYRUS

What, I? I shall go to Menedemus; I'll tell him she is a captive from Caria, rich, and of noble family; if he redeems her, there will be a considerable profit in this transaction.

CHREMES
You are in an error.

SYRUS
Why so?

CHREMES
I'll now answer you for Menedemus—I will not purchase her.

SYRUS
What is it you say? Do speak more agreeably to our wishes.

CHREMES
But there is no occasion.

SYRUS
No occasion?

CHREMES
Certainly not, i' faith.

SYRUS
How so, I wonder?

CHREMES
You shall soon know.[72]

SYRUS
Stop, stop; what is the reason that there is such a great noise at our door?

[They retire out of sight.

ACT THE FOURTH

SCENE I

Enter **SOSTRATA** and a **NURSE** in haste from the house of **CHREMES**, and **CHREMES** and **SYRUS** on the other side of the stage unperceived.

SOSTRATA [Holding up a ring and examining it]
Unless my fancy deceives me, surely this is the ring which I suspect it to be, the same with which my daughter was exposed.

CHREMES [Apart]
Syrus, what is the meaning of these expressions?

SOSTRATA
Nurse, how is it? Does it not seem to you the same?

NURSE
As for me, I said it was the same the very instant that you showed it me.

SOSTRATA
But have you now examined it thoroughly, my dear nurse?

NURSE
Thoroughly.

SOSTRATA
Then go in-doors at once, and if she has now done bathing, bring me word. I'll wait here in the mean time for my husband.

SYRUS [Apart]
She wants you, see what it is she wants; she is in a serious mood, I don't know why; it is not without a cause—I fear what it may be.

CHREMES
What it may be? I' faith, she'll now surely be announcing some important trifle, with a great parade.

SOSTRATA [Turning round]
Ha! my husband!

CHREMES
Ha! my wife!

SOSTRATA
I was looking for you.

CHREMES
Tell me what you want.

SOSTRATA
In the first place, this I beg of you, not to believe that I have ventured to do any thing contrary to your commands.

CHREMES
Would you have me believe you in this, although so incredible? Well, I will believe you.

SYRUS [Aside]
This excuse portends I know not what offense.

SOSTRATA

Do you remember me being pregnant, and yourself declaring to me, most peremptorily, that if I should bring forth a girl, you would not have it brought up.

CHREMES

I know what you have done, you have brought it up.

SYRUS [Aside]

Such is the fact, I'm sure: my young master has gained a loss[73] in consequence.

SOSTRATA

Not at all; but there was here an elderly woman of Corinth, of no indifferent character; to her I gave it to be exposed.

CHREMES

O Jupiter! that there should be such extreme folly in a person's mind.

SOSTRATA

Alas! what have I done?

CHREMES

And do you ask the question?

SOSTRATA

If I have acted wrong, my dear Chremes, I have done so in ignorance.

CHREMES

This, indeed, I know for certain, even if you were to deny it, that in every thing you both speak and act ignorantly and foolishly: how many blunders you disclose in this single affair! For, in the first place, then, if you had been disposed to obey my orders, the child ought to have been dispatched; you ought not in words to have feigned her death, and in reality to have left hopes of her surviving. But that I pass over; compassion, maternal affection, I allow it. But how finely you did provide for the future! What was your meaning? Do reflect. It's clear, beyond a doubt, that your daughter was betrayed by you to this old woman, either that through you she might make a living by her, or that she might be sold in open market as a slave. I suppose you reasoned thus: "any thing is enough, if only her life is saved:" what are you to do with those who understand neither law, nor right and justice? Be it for better or for worse, be it for them or against them, they see nothing except just what they please.

SOSTRATA

My dear Chremes, I have done wrong, I own; I am convinced. Now this I beg of you; inasmuch as you are more advanced in years than I, be so much the more ready to forgive; so that your justice may be some protection for my weakness.

CHREMES

I'll readily forgive you doing this, of course; but, Sostrata, my easy temper prompts you to do amiss. But, whatever this circumstance is, by reason of which this was begun upon, proceed to tell it.

SOSTRATA

As we women are all foolishly and wretchedly superstitious, when I delivered the child to her to be exposed, I drew a ring from off my finger, and ordered her to expose it, together with the child; that if she should die, she might not be without[74] some portion of our possessions.

CHREMES
That was right; thereby you proved the saving of yourself and her.[75]

SOSTRATA [Holding out the ring]
This is that ring.

CHREMES
Whence did you get it?

SOSTRATA
From the young woman whom Bacchis brought here with her.

SYRUS [Aside]
Ha!

CHREMES
What does she say?

SOSTRATA
She gave it me to keep for her, while she went to bathe. At first I paid no attention to it; but after I looked at it, I at once recognized it, and came running to you.

CHREMES
What do you suspect now, or have you discovered, relative to her?

SOSTRATA
I don't know; unless you inquire of herself whence she got it, if that can possibly be discovered.

SYRUS [Aside]
I'm undone! I see more hopes[76] from this incident than I desire. If it is so, she certainly must be ours.

CHREMES
Is this woman living to whom you delivered the child?

SOSTRATA
I don't know.

CHREMES
What account did she bring you at the time?

SOSTRATA
That she had done as I had ordered her.

CHREMES

Tell me what is the woman's name, that she may be inquired after.

SOSTRATA
Philtere.

SYRUS [Aside]
'Tis the very same. It's a wonder if she isn't found, and I lost.

CHREMES
Sostrata, follow me this way in-doors.

SOSTRATA
How much beyond my hopes has this matter turned out! How dreadfully afraid I was, Chremes, that you would now be of feelings as unrelenting as formerly you were on exposing the child.

CHREMES
Many a time a man can not be[77] such as he would be, if circumstances do not admit of it. Time has now so brought it about, that I should be glad of a daughter; formerly I wished for nothing less.

[**CHREMES** and **SOSTRATA** go into the house.

SCENE II

SYRUS alone.

SYRUS
Unless my fancy deceives me,[78] retribution[79] will not be very, far off from me; so much by this incident are my forces now utterly driven into straits; unless I contrive by some means that the old man mayn't come to know that this damsel is his son's mistress. For as to entertaining any hopes about the money, or supposing I could cajole him, it's useless; I shall be sufficiently triumphant, if I'm allowed to escape with my sides covered.[80] I'm vexed that such a tempting morsel has been so suddenly snatched away from my jaws. What am I to do? Or what shall I devise? I must begin upon my plan over again. Nothing is so difficult, but that it may be found out by seeking. What now if I set about it after this fashion.
[He considers]
That's of no use. What, if after this fashion? I effect just about the same. But this I think will do. It can not. Yes! excellent. Bravo! I've found out the best of all—I' faith, I do believe that after all I shall lay hold of this same runaway money.[81]

SCENE III

Enter **CLINIA** at the other side of the stage.

CLINIA [To himself]

Nothing can possibly henceforth befall me of such consequence as to cause me uneasiness; so extreme is this joy that has surprised me. Now then I shall give myself up entirely to my father, to be more frugal than even he could wish.

SYRUS [Apart]
I wasn't mistaken; she has been discovered, so far as I understand from these words of his.
[Advancing]
I am rejoiced that this matter has turned out for you so much to your wish.

CLINIA
O my dear Syrus, have you heard of it, pray?

SYRUS
How shouldn't I, when I was present all the while?

CLINIA
Did you ever hear of any thing falling out so fortunately for any one?

SYRUS
Never.

CLINIA
And, so may the Gods prosper me, I do not now rejoice so much on my own account as hers, whom I know to be deserving of any honor.

SYRUS
I believe it: but now, Clinia, come, attend to me in my turn. For your friend's business as well,—it must be seen to—that it is placed in a state of security, lest the old gentleman should now come to know any thing about his mistress.

CLINIA
O Jupiter!

SYRUS
Do be quiet.

CLINIA
My Antiphila will be mine.

SYRUS
Do you still interrupt me thus?

CLINIA
What can I do? My dear Syrus, I'm transported with joy! Do bear with me.

SYRUS
I' faith, I really do bear with you.

CLINIA
We are blest with the life of the Gods.

SYRUS
I'm taking pains to no purpose, I doubt.

CLINIA
Speak; I hear you.

SYRUS
But still you'll not mind it.

CLINIA
I will.

SYRUS
This must be seen to, I say, that your friend's business as well is placed in a state of security. For if you now go away from us, and leave Bacchis here, our old man will immediately come to know that she is Clitipho's mistress; if you take her away with you, it will be concealed just as much as it has been hitherto concealed.

CLINIA
But still, Syrus, nothing can make more against my marriage than this; for with what face am I to address my father about it? You understand what I mean?

SYRUS
Why not?

CLINIA
What can I say? What excuse can I make?

SYRUS
Nay, I don't want you to dissemble; tell him the whole case just as it really is.

CLINIA
What is it you say?

SYRUS
I bid you do this; tell him that you are in love with her, and want her for a wife: that this Bacchis is Clitipho's mistress.

CLINIA
You require a thing that is fair and reasonable, and easy to be done. And I suppose, then, you would have me request my father to keep it a secret from your old man.

SYRUS
On the contrary; to tell him directly the matter just as it is.

CLINIA

What? Are you quite in your senses or sober? Why, you were for ruining him outright. For how could he be in a state of security? Tell me that.

SYRUS

For my part, I yield the palm to this device. Here I do pride myself exultingly, in having in myself such exquisite resources, and power of address so great, as to deceive them both by telling the truth: so that when your old man tells ours that she is his son's mistress, he'll still not believe him.

CLINIA

But yet, by these means you again cut off all hopes of my marriage; for as long as Chremes believes that she is my mistress, he'll not give me his daughter. Perhaps you care little what becomes of me, so long as you provide for him.

SYRUS

What the plague, do you suppose I want this pretense to be kept up for an age? 'Tis but for a single day, only till I have secured the money: you be quiet; I ask no more.

CLINIA

Is that sufficient? If his father should come to know of it, pray, what then?

SYRUS

What if I have recourse to those who say, "What now if the sky were to fall?"[82]

CLINIA

I'm afraid to go about it.

SYRUS

You, afraid! As if it was not in your power to clear yourself at any time you like, and discover the whole matter.

CLINIA

Well, well; let Bacchis be brought over to our house.

SYRUS

Capital! she is coming out of doors.

SCENE IV

Enter **BACCHIS** and **PHRYGIA**, from the house of **CHREMES**.

BACCHIS [Pretending not to see **CLINIA** and **SYRUS**]

To a very fine purpose,[83] upon my faith, have the promises of Syrus brought me hither, who agreed to lend me ten minæ. If now he deceives me, oft as he may entreat me to come, he shall come in vain. Or else, when I've promised to come, and fixed the time, when he has carried word back for certain, and

Clitipho is on the stretch of expectation, I'll disappoint him and not come. Syrus will make atonement to me with his back.

CLINIA [Apart, to **SYRUS**]
She promises you very fairly.

SYRUS [To **CLINIA**]
But do you think she is in jest? She'll do it, if I don't take care.

BACCHIS [Aside]
They're asleep[84]—I'faith, I'll rouse them.
[Aloud]
My dear Phrygia, did you hear about the country-seat of Charinus, which that man was showing us just now?

PHRYGIA
I heard of it.

BACCHIS [Aloud]
That it was the next to the farm here on the right-hand side.[85]

PHRYGIA
I remember.

BACCHIS [Aloud]
Run thither post-haste; the Captain is keeping the feast of Bacchus[86] at his house.

SYRUS [Apart]
What is she going to be at?

BACCHIS [Aloud]
Tell him I am here very much against my inclination, and am detained; but that by some means or other I'll give them the slip and come to him.

[**PHRYGIA** moves.

SYRUS [Coming forward]
Upon my faith, I'm ruined! Bacchis, stay, stay; prithee, where are you sending her? Order her to stop.

BACCHIS [To **PHRYGIA**]
Be off.

SYRUS
Why, the money's ready.

BACCHIS
Why, then I'll stay.

[**PHRYGIA** returns.

SYRUS
And it will be given you presently.

BACCHIS
Just when you please; do I press you?

SYRUS
But do you know what you are to do, pray?

BACCHIS
What?

SYRUS
You must now go over to the house of Menedemus, and your equipage must be taken over thither.

BACCHIS
What scheme are you upon, you rascal?

SYRUS
What, I? Coining money to give you.

BACCHIS
Do you think me a proper person for you to play upon?

SYRUS
It's not without a purpose.

BACCHIS [Pointing to the house]
Why, have I any business then with you here?

SYRUS
O no; I'm only going to give you what's your own.

BACCHIS
Then let's be going.[87]

SYRUS
Follow this way.
[Goes to the door of **MENEDEMUS**, and calls]
Ho there! Dromo.

[Enter **DROMO** from the house.

DROMO
Who is it wants me?

SYRUS
Syrus.

DROMO
What's the matter?

SYRUS
Take over all the attendants of Bacchis to your house here immediately.

DROMO
Why so?

SYRUS
Ask no questions. Let them take what they brought here with them. The old gentleman will hope his expenses are lightened by their departure; for sure he little knows how much loss this trifling gain will bring him. You, Dromo, if you are wise, know nothing of what you do know.

DROMO
You shall own that I'm dumb.

[**CLINIA**, **BACCHIS**, and **PHRYGIA** go into the house of **MENEDEMUS**, and **DROMO** follows with **BACCHIS'S** retinue and baggage.

SCENE V

Enter **CHREMES** from his house.

CHREMES [To himself]
So may the Deities prosper me, I am now concerned for the fate of Menedemus, that so great a misfortune should have befallen him. To be maintaining that woman with such a retinue! Although I am well aware he'll not be sensible of it for some days to come, his son was so greatly missed by him; but when he sees such a vast expense incurred by him every day at home, and no limit to it, he'll wish that this son would leave him a second time. See—here comes Syrus most opportunely.

SYRUS [To himself, as he comes forward]
Why delay to accost him?

CHREMES
Syrus.

SYRUS
Well.

CHREMES
How go matters?

SYRUS

I've been wishing for some time for you to be thrown in my way.

CHREMES

You seem, then, to have effected something, I know not what, with the old gentleman.

SYRUS

As to what we were talking of a short time since? No sooner said than done.

CHREMES

In real earnest?

SYRUS

In real.

CHREMES

Upon my faith, I can not forbear patting your head for it. Come here, Syrus; I'll do you some good turn for this matter, and with pleasure.

[Patting his head.

SYRUS

But if you knew how cleverly it came into my head—

CHREMES

Pshaw! Do you boast because it has turned out according to your wishes?

SYRUS

On my word, not I, indeed; I am telling the truth.

CHREMES

Tell me how it is.

SYRUS

Clinia has told Menedemus, that this Bacchis is your Clitipho's mistress, and that he has taken her thither with him in order that you might not come to know of it.

CHREMES

Very good.

SYRUS

Tell me, please, what you think of it.

CHREMES

Extremely good, I declare.

SYRUS

Why yes, pretty fair. But listen, what a piece of policy still remains. He is then to say that he has seen your daughter—that her beauty charmed him as soon as he beheld her; and that he desires her for a wife.

CHREMES
What, her that has just been discovered?

SYRUS
The same; and, in fact, he'll request that she may be asked for.

CHREMES
For what purpose, Syrus? For I don't altogether comprehend it.

SYRUS
O dear, you are so dull.

CHREMES
Perhaps so.

SYRUS
Money will be given him for the wedding—with which golden trinkets and clothes—do you understand me?

CHREMES
To buy them—?

SYRUS
Just so.

CHREMES
But I neither give nor betroth my daughter to him.

SYRUS
But why?

CHREMES
Why, do you ask me? To a fellow—

SYRUS
Just as you please. I don't mean that in reality you should give her to him, but that you should pretend it.

CHREMES
Pretending is not in my way; do you mix up these plots of yours, so as not to mix me up in them. Do you think that I'll betroth my daughter to a person to whom I will not marry her?

SYRUS
I imagined so.

CHREMES

By no means.

SYRUS

It might have been cleverly managed; and I undertook this affair for the very reason, that a short time since you so urgently requested it.

CHREMES

I believe you.

SYRUS

But for my part, Chremes, I take it well and good, either way.

CHREMES

But still, I especially wish you to do your best for it to be brought about; but in some other way.

SYRUS

It shall be done: some other method must be thought of; but as to what I was telling you of,—about the money which she owes to Bacchis,—that must now be repaid her. And you will not, of course, now be having recourse to this method; "What have I to do with it? Was it lent to me? Did I give any orders? Had she the power to pawn my daughter without my consent?" They quote that saying, Chremes, with good reason, "Rigorous law[88] is often rigorous injustice."

CHREMES

I will not do so.

SYRUS

On the contrary, though others were at liberty, you are not at liberty; all think that you are in good and very easy circumstances.

CHREMES

Nay rather, I'll at once carry it to her myself.

SYRUS

Why no; request your son in preference.

CHREMES

For what reason?

SYRUS

Why, because the suspicion of being in love with her has been transferred to him with Menedemus.

CHREMES

What then?

SYRUS

Because it will seem to be more like probability when he gives it her; and at the same time I shall effect more easily what I wish. Here he comes too; go, and bring out the money.

CHREMES
I'll bring it.

[Goes into his house.

SCENE VI

Enter **CLITIPHO**.

CLITIPHO [To himself]
There is nothing so easy but that it becomes difficult when you do it with reluctance. As this walk of mine, for instance, though not fatiguing, it has reduced me to weariness. And now I dread nothing more than that I should be packed off somewhere hence once again, that I may not have access to Bacchis. May then all the Gods and Goddesses, as many as exist, confound you, Syrus, with these stratagems and plots of yours. You are always devising something of this kind, by means of which to torture me.

SYRUS
Will you not away with you—to where you deserve? How nearly had your forwardness proved my ruin!

CLITIPHO
Upon my faith, I wish it had been so; just what you deserve.

SYRUS
Deserve? How so? Really, I'm glad that I've heard this from you before you had the money which I was just going to give you.

CLITIPHO
What then would you have me to say to you? You've made a fool of me; brought my mistress hither, whom I'm not allowed to touch—

SYRUS
Well, I'm not angry then. But do you know where Bacchis is just now?

CLITIPHO
At our house.

SYRUS
No.

CLITIPHO
Where then?

SYRUS

At Clinia's.

CLITIPHO
I'm ruined!

SYRUS
Be of good heart; you shall presently carry to her the money that you promised her.

CLITIPHO
You do prate away.—Where from?

SYRUS
From your own father.

CLITIPHO
Perhaps you are joking with me.

SYRUS
The thing itself will prove it.

CLITIPHO
Indeed, then, I am a lucky man. Syrus, I do love you from my heart.

SYRUS
But your father's coming out. Take care not to express surprise at any thing, for what reason it is done; give way at the proper moment; do what he orders, and say but little.

SCENE VII

Enter **CHREMES** from the house, with a bag of money.

CHREMES
Where's Clitipho now?

SYRUS [Aside to **CLITIPHO**]
Say—here I am.

CLITIPHO
Here am I.

CHREMES [To **SYRUS**]
Have you told him how it is?

SYRUS
I've told him pretty well every thing.

CHREMES
Take this money, and carry it.

[Holding out the bag.

SYRUS [Aside to **CLITIPHO**]
Go—why do you stand still, you stone; why don't you take it?

CLITIPHO
Very well, give it me.

[Receives the bag.

SYRUS [To **CLITIPHO**]
Follow me this way directly.
[To **CHREMES**]
You in the mean while will wait here for us till we return; for there's no occasion for us to stay there long.

[**CLITIPHO** and **SYRUS** go into the house of **MENEDEMUS**.

CHREMES [To himself]
My daughter, in fact, has now had ten minæ from me, which I consider as paid for her board; another ten will follow these for clothes; and then she will require two talents for her portion. How many things, both just and unjust, are sanctioned by custom![89] Now I'm obliged, neglecting my business, to look out for some one on whom to bestow my property, that has been acquired by my labor.

SCENE VIII

Enter **MENEDEMUS** from his house.

MENEDEMUS [To **CLINIA** within]
My son, I now think myself the happiest of all men, since I find that you have returned to a rational mode of life.

CHREMES [Aside]
How much he is mistaken!

MENEDEMUS
Chremes, you are the very person I wanted; preserve, so far as in you lies, my son, myself, and my family.

CHREMES
Tell me what you would have me do.

MENEDEMUS

You have this day found a daughter.

CHREMES
What then?

MENEDEMUS
Clinia wishes her to be given him for a wife.

CHREMES
Prithee, what kind of a person are you?

MENEDEMUS
Why?

CHREMES
Have you already forgotten what passed between us, concerning a scheme, that by that method some money might be got out of you?

MENEDEMUS
I remember.

CHREMES
That self-same thing they are now about.

MENEDEMUS
What do you tell me, Chremes? Why surely, this Courtesan, who is at my house, is Clitipho's mistress.

CHREMES
So they say, and you believe it all; and they say that he is desirous of a wife, in order that, when I have betrothed her, you may give him money, with which to provide gold trinkets and clothing, and other things that are requisite.

MENEDEMUS
That is it, no doubt; that money will be given to his mistress.

CHREMES
Of course it is to be given.

MENEDEMUS
Alas! in vain then, unhappy man, have I been overjoyed; still however, I had rather any thing than be deprived of him. What answer now shall I report from you, Chremes, so that he may not perceive that I have found it out, and take it to heart?

CHREMES
To heart, indeed! you are too indulgent to him, Menedemus.

MENEDEMUS
Let me go on; I have now begun: assist me in this throughout, Chremes.

CHREMES
Say then, that you have seen me, and have treated about the marriage.

MENEDEMUS
I'll say so—what then?

CHREMES
That I will do every thing; that as a son-in-law he meets my approbation; in fine, too, if you like, tell him also that she has been promised him.

MENEDEMUS
Well, that's what I wanted—

CHREMES
That he may the sooner ask of you, and you may as soon as possible give him what you wish.

MENEDEMUS
It is my wish.

CHREMES
Assuredly, before very long, according as I view this matter, you'll have enough of him. But, however that may be, if you are wise, you'll give to him cautiously, and a little at a time.

MENEDEMUS
I'll do so.

CHREMES
Go in-doors and see how much he requires. I shall be at home, if you should want me for any thing.

MENEDEMUS
I certainly do want you; for I shall let you know whatever I do.

[They go into their respective houses.]

SCENE I

Enter **MENEDEMUS** from his house.

MENEDEMUS [To himself]
I am quite aware that I am not so overwise, or so very quick-sighted; but this assistant, prompter, and director[90] of mine, Chremes, outdoes me in that. Any one of those epithets which are applied to a fool is suited to myself, such as dolt, post, ass,[91] lump of lead; to him not one can apply; his stupidity surpasses them all.

[Enter **CHREMES**, speaking to **SOSTRATA** within.

CHREMES
Hold now, do, wife, leave off dinning the Gods with thanksgivings that your daughter has been discovered; unless you judge of them by your own disposition, and think that they understand nothing, unless the same thing has been told them a hundred times. But, in the mean time, why does my son linger there so long with Syrus?

MENEDEMUS
What persons do you say are lingering?

CHREMES
Ha! Menedemus, you have come opportunely. Tell me, have you told Clinia what I said?

MENEDEMUS
Every thing.

CHREMES
What did he say?

MENEDEMUS
He began to rejoice, just like people do who wish to be married.

CHREMES [Laughing]
Ha! ha! ha!

MENEDEMUS
Why are you laughing?

CHREMES
The sly tricks of my servant, Syrus, just came into my mind.

MENEDEMUS
Did they?

CHREMES
The rogue can even mould the countenances of people.[92]

MENEDEMUS
That my son is pretending that he is overjoyed, is it that you mean?

CHREMES [Laughing]
Just so.

MENEDEMUS
The very same thing came into my mind.

CHREMES

A crafty knave!

MENEDEMUS

Still more would you think such to be the fact, if you knew more.

CHREMES

Do you say so?

MENEDEMUS

Do you give attention then?

CHREMES

Just stop—first I want to know this, what money you have squandered; for when you told your son that she was promised, of course Dromo would at once throw in a word that golden jewels, clothes, and attendants would be needed for the bride, in order that you might give the money.

MENEDEMUS

No.

CHREMES

How, no?

MENEDEMUS

No, I tell you.

CHREMES

Nor yet your son himself?

MENEDEMUS

Not in the slightest, Chremes. He was only the more pressing on this one point, that the match might be concluded to-day.

CHREMES

You say what's surprising. What did my servant Syrus do? Didn't even he say any thing?

MENEDEMUS

Nothing at all.

CHREMES

For what reason, I don't know.

MENEDEMUS

For my part, I wonder at that, when you know other things so well. But this same Syrus has moulded your son,[93] too, to such perfection, that there could not be even the slightest suspicion that she is Clinia's mistress!

CHREMES

What do you say?

MENEDEMUS
Not to mention, then, their kissing and embracing; that I count nothing.

CHREMES
What more could be done to carry on the cheat?

MENEDEMUS
Pshaw!

CHREMES
What do you mean?

MENEDEMUS
Only listen. In the inner part of my house there is a certain room at the back; into this a bed was brought, and was made up with bed-clothes.

CHREMES
What took place after this?

MENEDEMUS
No sooner said than done, thither went Clitipho.

CHREMES
Alone?

MENEDEMUS
Alone.

CHREMES
I'm alarmed.

MENEDEMUS
Bacchis followed directly.

CHREMES
Alone?

MENEDEMUS
Alone.

CHREMES
I'm undone!

MENEDEMUS
When they had gone into the room, they shut the door.

CHREMES
Well—did Clinia see all this going on?

MENEDEMUS
How shouldn't he? He was with me.

CHREMES
Bacchis is my son's mistress, Menedemus—I'm undone.

MENEDEMUS
Why so?

CHREMES
I have hardly substance to suffice for ten days.[94]

MENEDEMUS
What! are you alarmed at it, because he is paying attention to his friend?

CHREMES
His "she-friend" rather.[95]

MENEDEMUS
If he really is paying it.

CHREMES
Is it a matter of doubt to you? Do you suppose that there is any person of so accommodating and tame a spirit as to suffer his own mistress, himself looking on, to—

MENEDEMUS [Chuckling and speaking ironically]
Why not? That I may be imposed upon the more easily.

CHREMES
Do you laugh at me? You have good reason. How angry I now am with myself! How many things gave proof, whereby, had I not been a stone, I might have been fully sensible of this? What was it I saw? Alas! wretch that I am! But assuredly they shall not escape my vengeance if I live; for this instant—

MENEDEMUS
Can you not contain yourself? Have you no respect for yourself? Am I not a sufficient example to you?

CHREMES
For very anger, Menedemus, I am not myself.

MENEDEMUS
For you to talk in that manner! Is it not a shame for you to be giving advice to others, to show wisdom abroad and yet be able to do nothing for yourself?

CHREMES
What shall I do?

MENEDEMUS

That which you said I failed to do: make him sensible that you are his father; make him venture to intrust every thing to you, to seek and to ask of you; so that he may look for no other resources and forsake you.[96]

CHREMES

Nay, I had much rather he would go any where in the world, than by his debaucheries here reduce his father to beggary! For if I go on supplying his extravagance, Menedemus, in that case my circumstances will undoubtedly be soon reduced to the level of your rake.

MENEDEMUS

What evils you will bring upon yourself in this affair, if you don't act with caution! You'll show yourself severe, and still pardon him at last; that too with an ill grace.

CHREMES

Ah! you don't know how vexed I am.

MENEDEMUS

Just as you please. What about that which I desire—that she may be married to my son? Unless there is any other step that you would prefer.

CHREMES

On the contrary, both the son-in-law and the connection are to my taste.

MENEDEMUS

What portion shall I say that you have named for your daughter? Why are you silent?

CHREMES

Portion?

MENEDEMUS

I say so.

CHREMES

Alas!

MENEDEMUS

Chremes, don't be at all afraid to speak, if it is but a small one. The portion is no consideration at all with us.

CHREMES

I did think that two talents were sufficient, according to my means. But if you wish me to be saved, and my estate and my son, you must say to this effect, that I have settled all my property on her as her portion.

MENEDEMUS

What scheme are you upon?

CHREMES

Pretend that you wonder at this, and at the same time ask him the reason why I do so.

MENEDEMUS

Why, really, I can't conceive the reason for your doing so.

CHREMES

Why do I do so? To check his feelings, which are now hurried away by luxury and wantonness, and to bring him down so as not to know which way to turn himself.

MENEDEMUS

What is your design?

CHREMES

Let me alone, and give me leave to have my own way in this matter.

MENEDEMUS

I do give you leave: is this your desire?

CHREMES

It is so.

MENEDEMUS

Then be it so.

CHREMES

And now let your son prepare to fetch the bride. The other one shall be schooled in such language as befits children. But Syrus—

MENEDEMUS

What of him?

CHREMES

What? If I live, I will have him so handsomely dressed, so well combed out, that he shall always remember me as long as he lives; to imagine that I'm to be a laughing-stock and a plaything for him! So may the Gods bless me! he would not have dared to do to a widow-woman the things which he has done to me.[97]

[They go into their respective houses.

SCENE II

Enter **MENEDEMUS**, with **CLITIPHO** and **SYRUS**.

CLITIPHO

Prithee, is it really the fact, Menedemus, that my father can, in so short a space of time, have cast off all the natural affection of a parent for me? For what crime? What so great enormity have I, to my misfortune, committed? Young men generally do the same.

MENEDEMUS

I am aware that this must be much more harsh and severe to you, on whom it falls; but yet I take it no less amiss than you. How it is so I know not, nor can I account for it, except that from my heart I wish you well.

CLITIPHO

Did not you say that my father was waiting here?

[Enter **CHREMES** from his house.

MENEDEMUS

See, here he is.

[**MENEDEMUS** goes into his house.

CHREMES

Why are you blaming me, Clitipho? Whatever I have done in this matter, I had a view to you and your imprudence. When I saw that you were of a careless disposition, and held the pleasures of the moment of the first importance, and did not look forward to the future, I took measures that you might neither want nor be able to waste this which I have. When, through your own conduct, it was not allowed me to give it you, to whom I ought before all, I had recourse to those who were your nearest relations; to them I have made over and intrusted every thing.[98] There you'll always find a refuge for your folly; food, clothing, and a roof under which to betake yourself.

CLITIPHO

Ah me!

CHREMES

It is better than that, you being my heir, Bacchis should possess this estate of mine.

SYRUS [Apart]

I'm ruined irrevocably!—Of what mischief have I, wretch that I am, unthinkingly been the cause?

CLITIPHO

Would I were dead!

CHREMES

Prithee, first learn what it is to live. When you know that, if life displeases you, then try the other.

SYRUS

Master, may I be allowed—?

CHREMES

Say on.

SYRUS
But may I safely?

CHREMES
Say on.

SYRUS
What injustice or what madness is this, that that in which I have offended, should be to his detriment?

CHREMES
It's all over.[99] Don't you mix yourself up in it; no one accuses you, Syrus, nor need you look out for an altar,[100] or for an intercessor for yourself.

SYRUS
What is your design?

CHREMES
I am not at all angry either with you—
[To **SYRUS**]
—or with you
[To **CLITIPHO**]
—nor is it fair that you should be so with me for what I am doing.

[He goes into his house.

SYRUS
He's gone. I wish I had asked him—

CLITIPHO
What, Syrus?

SYRUS
Where I am to get my subsistence; he has so utterly cast us adrift. You are to have it, for the present, at your sister's, I find.

CLITIPHO
Has it then come to this pass, Syrus—that I am to be in danger even of starving?

SYRUS
So we only live, there's hope—

CLITIPHO
What hope?

SYRUS
That we shall be hungry enough.

CLITIPHO
Do you jest in a matter so serious, and not give me any assistance with your advice?

SYRUS
On the contrary, I'm both now thinking of that, and have been about it all the time your father was speaking just now; and so far as I can perceive—

CLITIPHO
What?

SYRUS
It will not be wanting long.

[He meditates.

CLITIPHO
What is it, then?

SYRUS
It is this—I think that you are not their son.

CLITIPHO
How's that, Syrus? Are you quite in your senses?

SYRUS
I'll tell you what's come into my mind; be you the judge. While they had you alone, while they had no other source of joy more nearly to affect them, they indulged you, they lavished upon you. Now a daughter has been found, a pretense has been found in fact on which to turn you adrift.

CLITIPHO
It's very probable.

SYRUS
Do you suppose that he is so angry on account of this fault?

CLITIPHO
I do not think so.

SYRUS
Now consider another thing. All mothers are wont to be advocates for their sons when in fault, and to aid them against a father's severity; 'tis not so here.

CLITIPHO
You say true; what then shall I now do, Syrus?

SYRUS
Question them on this suspicion; mention the matter without reserve; either, if it is not true, you'll soon bring them both to compassion, or else you'll soon find out whose son you are.

CLITIPHO
You give good advice; I'll do so.

[He goes into the home of **CHREMES**.

SYRUS [To himself]
Most fortunately did this come into my mind. For the less hope the young man entertains, the greater the difficulty with which he'll bring his father to his own terms. I'm not sure even, that he may not take a wife, and then no thanks for Syrus. But what is this? The old man's coming out of doors; I'll be off. What has so far happened, I am surprised at, that he didn't order me to be carried off from here: now I'll away to Menedemus here, I'll secure him as my intercessor; I can put no trust in our old man.

[Goes into the house of **MENEDEMUS**.

SCENE III

Enter **CHREMES** and **SOSTRATA** from the house.

SOSTRATA
Really, sir, if you don't take care, you'll be causing some mischief to your son; and indeed I do wonder at it, my husband, how any thing so foolish could ever come into your head.

CHREMES
Oh, you persist in being the woman? Did I ever wish for any one thing in all my life, Sostrata, but that you were my contradicter on that occasion? And yet if I were now to ask you what it is that I have done amiss, or why you act thus, you would not know in what point you are now so obstinately opposing me in your folly.

SOSTRATA
I, not know?

CHREMES
Yes, rather, I should have said you do know; inasmuch as either expression amounts to the same thing.[101]

SOSTRATA
Alas! you are unreasonable to expect me to be silent in a matter of such importance.

CHREMES
I don't expect it; talk on then, I shall still do it not a bit the less.

SOSTRATA
Will you do it?

CHREMES

Certainly.

SOSTRATA
Don't you see how much evil you will be causing by that course?—He suspects himself to be a foundling.

CHREMES
Do you say so?

SOSTRATA
Assuredly it will be so.

CHREMES
Admit it.

SOSTRATA
Hold now—prithee, let that be for our enemies. Am I to admit that he is not my son who really is?

CHREMES
What! are you afraid that you can not prove that he is yours, whenever you please?

SOSTRATA
Because my daughter has been found?[102]

CHREMES
No; but for a reason why it should be much sooner believed—because he is just like you in disposition, you will easily prove that he is your child; for he is exactly like you; why, he has not a single vice left him but you have just the same. Then, besides, no woman could have been the mother of such a son but yourself. But he's coming out of doors, and how demure! When you understand the matter, you may form your own conclusions.

SCENE IV

Enter **CLITIPHO** from the house of **CHREMES**.

CLITIPHO
If there ever was any time, mother, when I caused you pleasure, being called your son by your own desire, I beseech you to remember it, and now to take compassion on me in my distress. A thing I beg and request—do discover to me my parents.

SOSTRATA
I conjure you, my son, not to entertain that notion in your mind, that you are another person's child.

CLITIPHO
I am.

SOSTRATA

Wretch that I am!
[Turning to **CHREMES**]
Was it this that you wanted, pray?
[To **CLITIPHO**]
So may you be the survivor of me and of him, you are my son and his; and henceforth, if you love me, take care that I never hear that speech from you again.

CHREMES
But I say, if you fear me, take care how I find these propensities existing in you.

CLITIPHO
What propensities?

CHREMES
If you wish to know, I'll tell you; being a trifler, an idler, a cheat, a glutton, a debauchee, a spendthrift— Believe me, and believe that you are our son.

CLITIPHO
This is not the language of a parent.

CHREMES
If you had been born from my head, Clitipho, just as they say Minerva was from Jove's, none the more on that account would I suffer myself to be disgraced by your profligacy.[103]

SOSTRATA
May the Gods forbid it.

CHREMES
I don't know as to the Gods;[104] so far as I shall be enabled, I will carefully prevent it. You are seeking that which you possess—parents; that which you are in want of you don't seek—in what way to pay obedience to a father, and to preserve what he acquired by his industry. That you by trickery should bring before my eyes—I am ashamed to mention the unseemly word in her presence—
[Pointing to SOSTRATA]
—but you were not in any degree ashamed to act thus.

CLITIPHO [Aside]
Alas! how thoroughly displeased I now am with myself! How much ashamed! nor do I know how to make a beginning to pacify him.

SCENE V

Enter **MENEDEMUS** from his house.

MENEDEMUS [To himself]
Why really, Chremes is treating his son too harshly and too unkindly. I'm come out, therefore, to make peace between them. Most opportunely I see them both.

CHREMES

Well, Menedemus, why don't you order my daughter to be sent for, and close with the offer[105] of the portion that I mentioned?

SOSTRATA

My husband, I entreat you not to do it.

CLITIPHO

Father, I entreat you to forgive me.

MENEDEMUS

Forgive him, Chremes; do let them prevail upon you.

CHREMES

Am I knowingly to make my property a present to Bacchis? I'll not do it.

MENEDEMUS

Why, we would not suffer it.

CLITIPHO

If you desire me to live, father, do forgive me.

SOSTRATA

Do, my dear Chremes.

MENEDEMUS

Come, Chremes, pray, don't be so obdurate.

CHREMES

What am I to do here? I see I am not allowed to carry this through, as I had intended.

MENEDEMUS

You are acting as becomes you.

CHREMES

On this condition, then, I'll do it; if he does that which I think it right he should do.

CLITIPHO

Father, I'll do any thing; command me.

CHREMES

You must take a wife.

CLITIPHO

Father—

CHREMES

I'll hear nothing.

MENEDEMUS
I'll take it upon myself; he shall do so.

CHREMES
I don't hear any thing from him as yet.

CLITIPHO [Aside]
I'm undone!

SOSTRATA
Do you hesitate, Clitipho?

CHREMES
Nay, just as he likes.

MENEDEMUS
He'll do it all.

SOSTRATA
This course, while you are making a beginning, is disagreeable, and while you are unacquainted with it. When you have become acquainted with it, it will become easy.

CLITIPHO
I'll do it, father.

SOSTRATA
My son, upon my honor I'll give you that charming girl, whom you may soon become attached to, the daughter of our neighbor Phanocrata.

CLITIPHO
What! that red-haired girl, with cat's eyes, freckled face,[106] and hooked nose? I can not, father.

CHREMES
Heyday! how nice he is! You would fancy he had set his mind upon it.

SOSTRATA
I'll name another.

CLITIPHO
Why no—since I must marry, I myself have one that I should pretty nearly make choice of.

SOSTRATA
Now, son, I commend you.

CLITIPHO
The daughter of Archonides here.

SOSTRATA
I'm quite agreeable.

CLITIPHO
Father, this now remains.

CHREMES
What is it?

CLITIPHO
I want you to pardon Syrus for what he has done for my sake.

CHREMES
Be it so.
[To the **AUDIENCE**]
Fare you well, and grant us your applause.

FOOTNOTES

[Footnote 1: See the Dramatis Personæ of the Andria.]

[Footnote 2: From μενὸς, "strength," and δῆμος, "the people."]

[Footnote 3: From κλίνω, "to incline," or from κλινὴ, "the marriage-bed."]

[Footnote 4: From κλειτὸς, "illustrious," and φῶς, "light."]

[Footnote 5: See the Dramatis Personæ of the Andria.]

[Footnote 6: From Syria, his native country.]

[Footnote 7: From σώζω, "to preserve," or "save."]

[Footnote 8: From ἀντὶ, "in return," and φιλῶ, "to love."]

[Footnote 9: From Bacchus, the God of Wine.]

[Footnote 10: From Phrygia, her native country.]

[Footnote 11: Being Consuls]—M. Juventius Thalna and Ti. Sempronius Gracchus were Consuls in the year from the Building of the City 589, and B.C. 164.]

[Footnote 12: Assigned to an old man]—Ver. 1. He refers to the fact that the Prologue was in general spoken by young men, whereas it is here spoken by L. Ambivius Turpio, the leader of the Company, a man stricken in years. The Prologue was generally not recited by a person who performed a character in the opening Scene.]

[Footnote 13: That I will first explain to you]—Ver. 3. His meaning seems to be, that he will first tell them the reason why he, who is to take a part in the opening Scene, speaks the Prologue, which is usually spoken by a young man who does not take part in that Scene; and that he will then proceed to speak in character (eloquor), as Chremes, in the first Scene. His reason for being chosen to speak the Prologue, is that he may be a pleader (orator) for the Poet, a task which would be likely to be better performed by him than by a younger man.]

[Footnote 14: From an entire Greek one]—Ver. 4. In contradistinction to such Plays as the Andria, as to which it was a subject of complaint that it had been formed out of a mixture (contaminatus) of the Andrian and Perinthian of Menander.]

[Footnote 15: Which from a two-fold plot]—Ver. 6. Vollbehr suggests that the meaning of this line is, that though it is but one Play, it has a two-fold plot—the intrigues of two young men with two mistresses, and the follies of two old men. As this Play is supposed to represent the events of two successive days, the night intervening, it has been suggested that the reading is "duplex—ex argumento—simplici;" the Play is "two-fold, with but one plot," as extending to two successive days. The Play derives its name from the Greek words, ἑαυτὸν, "himself," and τιμωρουμενὸς, "tormenting."]

[Footnote 16: To be a Pleader]—Ver. 11. He is to be the pleader and advocate of the Poet, to influence the Audience in his favor, and against his adversaries; and not to explain the plot of the Play. Colman has the following observation: "It is impossible not to regret that there are not above ten lines of the Self-Tormentor preserved among the Fragments of Menander. We are so deeply interested by what we see of that character in Terence, that one can not but be curious to inquire in what manner the Greek Poet sustained it through five Acts. The Roman author, though he has adopted the title of the Greek Play, has so altered the fable, that Menedemus is soon thrown into the background, and Chremes is brought forward as the principal object; or, to vary the allusion a little, the Menedemus of Terence seems to be a drawing in miniature copied from a full length, as large as the life, by Menander."]

[Footnote 17: A malevolent old Poet]—Ver. 22. He alludes to his old enemy, Luscus Lavinius, referred to in the preceding Prologue.]

[Footnote 18: The genius of his friends]—Ver. 24. He alludes to a report which had been spread, that his friends Lælius and Scipio had published their own compositions under his name. Servilius is also mentioned by Eugraphius as another of his patrons respecting whom similar stories were circulated.]

[Footnote 19: As he ran alone in the street]—Ver. 31. He probably does not intend to censure this practice entirely in Comedy, but to remind the Audience that in some recent Play of Luscus Lavinius this had been the sole stirring incident introduced. Plautus introduces Mercury running in the guise of Sosia, in the fourth Scene of the Amphitryon, l. 987, and exclaiming, "For surely, why, faith, should I, a God, be any less allowed to threaten the public, if it doesn't get out of my way, than a slave in the Comedies?" This practice can not, however, be intended to be here censured by Plautus, as he is guilty of it in three other instances. In the Mercator, Acanthio runs to his master Charinus, to tell him that his mistress Pasicompsa has been seen in the ship by his father Demipho; in the Stichus, Pinacium, a slave, runs to inform his mistress Philumena that her husband has arrived in port, on his return from Asia; and in the Mostellaria, Tranio, in haste, brings information of the unexpected arrival of Theuropides. The "currens servus" is also mentioned in the Prologue to the Andria, l. 36. See the soliloquy of Stasimus, in the Trinummus of Plautus, l. 1007.]

[Footnote 20: A quiet Play]—Ver. 36. "Statariam." See the spurious Prologue to the Bacchides of Plautus, l. 10, and the Note to the passage in Bohn's Translation. The Comedy of the Romans was either "stataria", "motoria", or "mixta". "Stataria" was a Comedy which was calm and peaceable, such as the Cistellaria of Plautus; "motoria" was one full of action and disturbance, like his Amphitryon; while the "Comœdia mixta" was a mixture of both, such as the Eunuchus of Terence.]

[Footnote 21: What in each character]—Ver. 47. "In utramque partem ingenium quid possit meum." This line is entirely omitted in Vollbehr's edition; but it appears to be merely a typographical error.]

[Footnote 22: How little work is done here]—Ver. 72. Vollbehr thinks that his meaning is, that he is quite vexed to see so little progress made, in spite of his neighbor's continual vexation and turmoil, and that, as he says in the next line, he is of opinion that if he were to cease working himself, and were to overlook his servants, he would get far more done. It is more generally thought to be an objection which Chremes suggests that Menedemus may possibly make.]

[Footnote 23: I am a man]—Ver. 77. "Homo sum: humani nihil a me alienum puto." St. Augustine says, that at the delivery of this sentiment, the Theatre resounded with applause; and deservedly, indeed, for it is replete with the very essence of benevolence and disregard of self. Cicero quotes the passage in his work De Officiis, B. i., c. 9. The remarks of Sir Richard Steele upon this passage, in the Spectator, No. 502, are worthy to be transcribed at length. "The Play was the Self-Tormentor. It is from the beginning to the end a perfect picture of human life, but I did not observe in the whole one passage that could raise a laugh. How well-disposed must that people be, who could be entertained with satisfaction by so sober and polite mirth! In the first Scene of the Comedy, when one of the old men accuses the other of impertinence for interposing in his affairs, he answers, 'I am a man, and can not help feeling any sorrow that can arrive at man.' It is said this sentence was received with an universal applause. There can not be a greater argument of the general good understanding of a people, than their sudden consent to give their approbation of a sentiment which has no emotion in it. If it were spoken with ever so great skill in the actor, the manner of uttering that sentence could have nothing in it which could strike any but people of the greatest humanity—nay, people elegant and skillful in observation upon it. It is possible that he may have laid his hand on his heart, and with a winning insinuation in his countenance, expressed to his neighbor that he was a man who made his case his own; yet I will engage, a player in Covent Garden might hit such an attitude a thousand times before he would have been regarded."]

[Footnote 24: Take off my shoes]—Ver. 124. As to the "socci," or low shoes of the ancients, see the Notes to the Trinummus of Plautus, l. 720, in Bohn's Translation. It was the especial duty of certain slaves to take off the shoes of their masters.]

[Footnote 25: To spread the couches]—Ver. 125. The "lecti" or "couches" upon which the ancients reclined at meals, have been enlarged upon in the Notes to Plautus, where full reference is also made to the "coena" or "dinner," and other meals of the Romans.]

[Footnote 26: Provide me with dress]—Ver. 130. It was the custom for the mistress and female servants in each family to make the clothes of the master. Thus in the Fasti of Ovid, B. ii., l. 746, Lucretia is found amidst her female servants, making a cloak, or "lacerna," for her husband. Suetonius says that Augustus refused to wear any garments not woven by his female relations. Cooke seems to think that "vestiant" alludes to the very act of putting the clothes upon a person. He says, "The better sort of people had eating-dresses, which are here alluded to. These dresses were light garments, to put on as soon as they had bathed. They commonly bathed before eating, and the chief meal was in the evening." This, however, does not seem to be the meaning of the passage, although Colman has adopted it. We may here remark that the censure here described is not unlike that mentioned in the Prologue to the Mercator of Plautus, as administered by Demænetus to his son Charinus.]

[Footnote 27: Neither movables]—Ver. 141. "Vas" is here used as a general name for articles of furniture. This line appears to be copied almost literally from one of Menander, which still exists.]

[Footnote 28: To sell my house]—Ver. 145. On the mode of advertising houses to let or be sold among the Romans, see the Trinummus of Plautus, l. 168, and the Note to the passage in Bohn's Translation.]

[Footnote 29: Toward your children]—Ver. 151. The plural "liberos" is here used to signify the one son which Menedemus has. So in the Hecyra, l. 217, the same word is used to signify but one daughter. This was a common mode of expression in the times of the earlier Latin authors.]

[Footnote 30: Festival of Bacchus, "Dionysia"]—Ver. 162. It is generally supposed that there were four Festivals called the Dionysia, during the year, at Athens. The first was the Rural, or Lesser Dionysia, κατ᾽ ἀγροὺς, a vintage festival, which was celebrated in the "Demi" or boroughs of Attica, in honor of Bacchus, in the month Poseidon. This was the most ancient of the Festivals, and was held with the greatest merriment and freedom; the slaves then enjoyed the same amount of liberty as they did at the Saturnalia at Rome. The second Festival, which was called the Lensea, from ληνὸς, a wine-press, was celebrated in the month Gamelion, with Scenic contests in Tragedy and Comedy. The third Dionysian Festival was the Anthesteria, or "Spring feast," being celebrated during three days in the month Anthesterion. The first day was called πιϑοίγια, or "the Opening of the casks," as on that day the casks were opened to taste the wine of the preceding year. The second day was called χοες, from χοῦς, "a cup," and was probably devoted to drinking. The third day was called χυτροὶ, from χυτρὸς, "a pot," as on it persons offered pots with flower-seeds or cooked vegetables to Dionysus or Bacchus. The fourth Attic festival of Dionysius was celebrated in the month Elaphebolion, and was called the Dionysia ἐν ἄστει, Αστικὰ, or Μεγαλὰ, the "City" or "great" festival. It was celebrated with great magnificence, processions and dramatic representations forming part of the ceremonial. From Greece, by way of Sicily, the Bacchanalia, or festivals of Bacchus, were introduced into Rome, where they became the scenes of and pretext for every kind of vice and debauchery, until at length they were put down in the year B.C. 187, with a strong hand, by the Consuls Spurius Posthumius Albinus and Q. Marcius Philippus; from which period the words "bacchor" and "bacchator" became synonymous with the practice of every kind of vice and turpitude that could outrage common decency. See a very full account of the Dionysia and the Bacchanalia in Dr. Smith's Dictionary of Greek and Roman Antiquities.]

[Footnote 31: Is of service to him]—Ver. 199. He means that it is to the advantage of Clitipho that Clinia should be seen to stand in awe of his father.]

[Footnote 32: Reasonable men]—Ver. 205. "Homo," "a man," is here put for men in general who are fathers.]

[Footnote 33: Of knowing and of pardoning]—Ver. 218. There is a jingle intended here in the resemblance of the words "cognoscendi," "knowing," and "ignoscendi," "pardoning."]

[Footnote 34: Is—fair words]—Ver. 228. "Recte est." It is supposed that he pauses before uttering these words, which mean "very well," or "very good," implying the giving an assent without making a promise; he tells the reason, in saying that he has scruples or prejudices against confessing that he has got nothing to give her.]

[Footnote 35: Great way from here]—Ver. 239. That is, from the place where they are, in the country, to Athens.]

[Footnote 36: Troop of female attendants]—Ver. 245. The train and expenses of a courtesan of high station are admirably depicted in the speech of Lysiteles, in the Trinummus of Plautus, l. 252.]

[Footnote 37: In a mourning dress]—Ver. 286. Among the Greeks, in general, mourning for the dead seems to have lasted till the thirtieth day after the funeral, and during that period black dresses were worn. The Romans also wore mourning for the dead, which seems, in the time of the Republic, to have been black or dark blue for either sex. Under the Empire the men continued to wear black, but the women wore white. No jewels or ornaments were worn upon these occasions.]

[Footnote 38: With no worthless woman's trumpery]—Ver. 289. By "nullâ malâ re muliebri" he clearly means that they did not find her painted up with the cosmetics which some women were in the habit of using. Such preparations for the face as white-lead, wax, antimony, or vermilion, well deserve the name of "mala res." A host of these cosmetics will be found described in Ovid's Fragment "On the Care of the Complexion," and much information upon this subject is given in various passages in the Art of Love. In the Remedy of Love, l. 351, Ovid speaks of these practices in the following terms: "At the moment, too, when she shall be smearing her face with the cosmetics laid up on it, you may come into the presence of your mistress, and don't let shame prevent you. You will find there boxes, and a thousand colors of objects; and you will see 'oesypum,' the ointment of the fleece, trickling down and flowing upon her heated bosom. These drugs, Phineus, smell like thy tables; not once alone has sickness been caused by this to my stomach." Lucretius also, in his Fourth Book, l. 1168, speaks of a female who "covers herself with noxious odors, and whom her female attendants fly from to a distance, and chuckle by stealth." See also the Mostellaria of Plautus, Act I., Scene 3, l. 135, where Philematium is introduced making her toilet on the stage.]

[Footnote 39: Do hold your peace]—Ver. 291. "Pax," literally "peace!" in the sense of "Hush!" "Be quiet!" See the Notes to the Trinummus of Plautus, ll. 889-891, in Bohn's Translation.]

[Footnote 40: The woof]—Ver. 293. See an interesting passage on the ancient weaving, in the Metamorphoses of Ovid, B. vi., l. 54, et seq. See also the Epistle of Penelope to Ulysses, in the Heroides of Ovid, l. 10, and the Note in Bohn's English Translation.]

[Footnote 41: She was weaving]—Ver. 294. This line and part of the next are supposed to have been translated almost literally from some lines, the composition of Menander, which are still extant.]

[Footnote 42: Your Bacchis, whom we are bringing]—Ver. 310. Colman has the following remark: "Here we enter upon the other part of the table, which the Poet has most artfully complicated with the main subject by making Syrus bring Clitipho's mistress along with Antiphila. This part of the story, we know, was not in Menander."]

[Footnote 43: Incur this risk]—Ver. 337. As to his own mistress.]

[Footnote 44: Upon either ear]—Ver. 342. "In aurem utramvis," a proverbial expression, implying an easy and secure repose. It is also used by Plautus, and is found in a fragment of the Πλοκιὸν, or Necklace, a Comedy of Menander.]

[Footnote 45: Still do that which I said]—Ver. 346. "Perge porro, tamen istue ago." Stallbaum observes that the meaning is: "Although I'm going off, I'm still attending to what you're saying." According to Schmieder and others, it means: "Call on just as you please, I shall persist in sending Bacchis away."]

[Footnote 46: Such great people]—Ver. 363. "Quos," literally, "What persons!"]

[Footnote 47: Words of double meaning]—Ver. 372. "Inversa verba, eversas cervices tuas." "Inversa verba" clearly means, words with a double meaning, or substituted for others by previous arrangement, like correspondence by cipher. Lucretius uses the words in this sense, B. i., l. 643. A full account of the secret signs and correspondence in use among the ancients will be found in the 16th and 17th Epistles of the Heroides of Ovid, in his Amours, B. i., El. 4, and in various passages of the Art of Love. See also the Asinaria of Plautus, l. 780. It is not known for certain what "eversa cervix" here means; it may mean the turning of the neck in some particular manner by way of a hint or to give a sidelong look, or it may allude to the act of snatching a kiss on the sly, which might lead to a discovery.]

[Footnote 48: A man whose manners—those persons]—Ver. 393. "Cujus—hi;" a change of number by the use of the figure Enallage.]

[Footnote 49: I can scarce endure it]—Ver. 400. Colman has the following remark on this passage: "Madame Dacier, contrary to the authority of all editions and MSS., adopts a conceit of her father's in this place, and places this speech to Clitipho, whom she supposes to have retired to a hiding-place, where he might overhear the conversation, and from whence he peeps out to make this speech to Syrus. This she calls an agreeable jeu de théâtre, and doubts not but all lovers of Terence will be obliged to her father for so ingenious a remark; but it is to be feared that critical sagacity will not be so lavish of acknowledgments as filial piety. There does not appear the least foundation for this remark in the Scene, nor has the Poet given us the least room to doubt of Clitipho being actually departed. To me, instead of an agreeable jeu de théâtre, it appears a most absurd and ridiculous device; particularly vicious in this place, as it most injudiciously tends to interrupt the course of Clinia's more interesting passion, so admirably delineated in this little Scene."]

[Footnote 50: It is now daybreak]—Ver. 410. Though this is the only Play which includes more than one day in the action, it is not the only one in which the day is represented as breaking. The Amphitryon and the Curculio of Plautus commence before daybreak, and the action is carried on into the middle of the day. Madame Dacier absolutely considers it as a fact beyond all doubt, that the Roman Audience went home after the first two Acts of the Play, and returned for the representation of the third the next morning at daybreak. Scaliger was of the same opinion; but it is not generally entertained by Commentators.]

[Footnote 51: How I was affected]—Ver. 436. "Ut essem," literally, "How I was."]

[Footnote 52: If a satrap]—Ver. 452. "Satrapa" was a Persian word signifying "a ruler of a province." The name was considered as synonymous with "possessor of wealth almost inexhaustible."]

[Footnote 53: In tasting only]—Ver. 457. "Pytiso" was the name given to the nasty practice of tasting wine, and then spitting it out; offensive in a man, but infinitely more so in a woman. It seems in those times to have been done by persons who wished to give themselves airs in the houses of private persons; at the present day it is probably confined to wine-vaults and sale-rooms where wine is put up to auction, and even there it is practiced much more than is either necessary or agreeable. Doubtless Bacchis did it to show her exquisite taste in the matter of wines.]

[Footnote 54: Is too acid]—Ver. 458. "Asperum;" meaning that the wine was not old enough for her palate. The great fault of the Greek wines was their tartness, for which reason sea-water was mixed with them all except the Chian, which was the highest class of wine.]

[Footnote 55: Respected sir]—Ver. 459. "Pater," literally "father;" a title by which the young generally addressed aged persons who were strangers to them.]

[Footnote 56: All the casks, all the vessels]—Ver. 460. "Dolia omnia, omnes serias." The finer kinds of wine were drawn off from the "dolia," or large vessels, into the "amphoræ," which, like the "dolia," were made of earth, and sometimes of glass. The mouths of the vessels were stopped tight by a plug of wood or cork, which was made impervious to the atmosphere by being rubbed over with a composition of pitch, clay, wax, or gypsum. On the outside, the title of the wine was painted, and among the Romans the date of the vintage was denoted by the names of the Consuls then in office. When the vessels were of glass, small tickets or labels, called "pittacia," were suspended from them, stating to a similar effect. The "seriæ" were much the same as the "dolia," perhaps somewhat smaller; they were both long, bell-mouthed vessels of earthen-ware, formed of the best clay, and lined with pitch while hot from the furnace. "Seriæ" were also used to contain oil and other liquids; and in the Captivi of Plautus the word is applied to pans used for the purpose of salting meat. "Relino" signifies the act of taking the seal of pitch or wax off the stopper of the wine-vessel.]

[Footnote 57: With that servant of yours]—Ver. 473. Dromo.]

[Footnote 58: What an inlet]—Ver. 482. "Fenestram;" literally, "a window."]

[Footnote 59: This night with my eyes]—Ver. 491. Colman has the following Note here: "Hedelin obstinately contends from this passage, that neither Chremes nor any of his family went to bed the whole night; the contrary of which is evident, as Menage observes, from the two next Scenes. For why should Syrus take notice of his being up so early, if he had never retired to rest? Or would Chremes have reproached Clitipho for his behavior the night before, had the feast never been interrupted? Eugraphius's interpretation of these words is natural and obvious, who explains them to signify that the anxiety of Chremes to restore Clinia to Menedemus broke his rest."]

[Footnote 60: That they may not perceive]—Ver. 511. Madame Dacier observes that Chremes seizes this as a very plausible and necessary pretense to engage Menedemus to return home, and not to his labors in the field, as he had at first intended.]

[Footnote 61: Old age of an eagle]—Ver. 521. This was a proverbial expression, signifying a hale and vigorous old age. It has been suggested, too, that it alludes to the practice of some old men, who drink more than they eat. It was vulgarly said that eagles never die of old age, and that when, by reason of their beaks growing inward, they are unable to feed upon their prey, they live by sucking the blood.]

[Footnote 62: Not like those of former days]—Ver. 524. Syrus, by showing himself an admirer of the good old times, a "laudator temporis acti," is wishful to flatter the vanity of Chremes, as it is a feeling common to old age, perhaps by no means an unamiable one, to think former times better than the present. Aged people feel grateful to those happy hours when their hopes were bright, and every thing was viewed from the sunny side of life.]

[Footnote 63: Can no longer support her expenses]—Ver. 544. He refers to Menedemus and Bacchis.]

[Footnote 64: But in case, none the more]—Ver. 555. "Sed si quid, ne quid." An instance of Aposiopesis, signifying "But if any thing does happen, don't you blame me."]

[Footnote 65: And truly, Chremes]—Ver. 557. Some suppose that this is said in apparent candor by Syrus, in order the more readily to throw Chremes off his guard. Other Commentators, again, fancy these words to be said by Syrus in a low voice, aside, which seems not improbable; it being a just retribution on Chremes for his recommendation, however well intended: in that case, Chremes probably overhears it, if we may judge from his answer.]

[Footnote 66: 'Tis the truth]—Ver. 568. "Factum." "Done for" is another translation which this word will here admit of.]

[Footnote 67: That he does the same]—Ver. 577. Clinia.]

[Footnote 68: Of a prudent and discreet person]—Ver. 580. This is said ironically.]

[Footnote 69: Is there but one way]—Ver. 583. And that an immodest one.]

[Footnote 70: With your wife]—Ver. 604. Madame Dacier remarks, that as Antiphila is shortly to be acknowledged as the daughter of Chremes, she is not therefore in company with the other women at the feast, who are Courtesans, but with the wife of Chremes, and consequently free from reproach or scandal.]

[Footnote 71: Would she really be a security]—Ver. 606. The question of Chremes seems directed to the fact whether the girl is of value sufficient to be good security for the thousand drachmæ.]

[Footnote 72: You shall soon know]—Ver. 612. Madame Dacier suggests that Chremes is prevented by his wife's coming from making a proposal to advance the money himself, on the supposition that it will be a lucrative speculation. This notion is contradicted by Colman, who adds the following note from Eugraphius: "Syrus pretends to have concerted this plot against Menedemus, in order to trick him out of some money to be given to Clinia's supposed mistress. Chremes, however, does not approve of this: yet it serves to carry on the plot; for when Antiphila proves afterward to be the daughter of Chremes, he necessarily becomes the debtor of Bacchis, and is obliged to lay down the sum for which he imagines his daughter is pledged."]

[Footnote 73: Has gained a loss]—Ver. 628. He alludes to Clitipho, who, by the discovery of his sister, would not come in for such a large share of his father's property, and would consequently, as Syrus observes, gain a loss.]

[Footnote 74: That she might not be without]—Ver. 652. Madame Dacier observes upon this passage, that the ancients thought themselves guilty of a heinous offense if they suffered their children to die without having bestowed on them some of their property; it was consequently the custom of the women, before exposing children, to attach to them some jewel or trinket among their clothes, hoping thereby to avoid incurring the guilt above mentioned, and to ease their consciences.]

[Footnote 75: Saving of yourself and her]—Ver. 653. Madame Dacier says that the meaning of this passage is this: Chremes tells his wife that by having given this ring, she has done two good acts instead of one—she has both cleared her conscience and saved the child; for had there been no ring or token exposed with the infant, the finder would not have been at the trouble of taking care of it, but might have left it to perish, never suspecting it would be inquired after, or himself liberally rewarded for having preserved it.]

[Footnote 76: I see more hopes]—Ver. 659. Syrus is now alarmed that Antiphila should so soon be acknowledged as the daughter of Chremes, lest he may lose the opportunity of obtaining the money, and be punished as well, in case the imposition is detected, and Bacchis discovered to be the mistress of Clitipho and not of Clinia.]

[Footnote 77: A man can not be]—Ver. 666. This he says by way of palliating the cruelty he was guilty of in his orders to have the child put to death.]

[Footnote 78: Unless my fancy deceives me]—Ver. 668. "Nisi me animus fallit." He comically repeats the very same words with which Sostrata commenced in the last Scene.]

[Footnote 79: Retribution]—Ver. 668. "Infortunium!" was the name by which the slaves commonly denoted a beating. Colman has the following remark here: "Madame Dacier, and most of the later critics who have implicitly followed her, tell us that in the interval between the third and fourth Acts, Syrus has been present at the interview between Chremes and Antiphila within. The only difficulty in this doctrine is how to reconcile it to the apparent ignorance of Syrus, which he discovers at the entrance of Clinia. But this objection, says she, is easily answered. Syrus having partly heard Antiphila's story, and finding things likely to take an unfavorable turn, retires to consider what is best to be done. But surely this is a most unnatural impatience at so critical a conjuncture; and, after all, would it not be better to take up the matter just where Terence has left it, and to suppose that Syrus knew nothing more of the affair than what might be collected from the late conversation between Chremes and Sostrata, at which we know he was present? This at once accounts for his apprehensions, which he betrayed even during that Scene, as well as for his imperfect knowledge of the real state of the case, till apprised of the whole by Clinia."]

[Footnote 80: With my sides covered]—Ver. 673. He most probably alludes to the custom of tying up the slaves by their hands, after stripping them naked, when of course their "latera" or "sides" would be exposed, and come in for a share of the lashes.]

[Footnote 81: Runaway money]—Ver. 678. "Fugitivum argentum." Madame Dacier suggests that this is a bad translation of the words of Menander, which were "ἀποστρέψειν τὸν δραπέταν χρυσὸν" where "χρυσὸς" signified both "gold" and the name of a slave.]

[Footnote 82: If the sky were to fall]—Ver. 719. He means those who create unnecessary difficulties in their imagination. Colman quotes the following remark from Patrick: "There is a remarkable passage in Arrian's Account of Alexander, lib. iv., where he tells us that some embassadors from the Celtic, being asked by Alexander what in the world they dreaded most, answered, 'That they feared lest the sky should fall [upon them].' Alexander, who expected to hear himself named, was surprised at an answer which signified that they thought themselves beyond the reach of all human power, plainly implying that nothing could hurt them, unless he would suppose impossibilities, or a total destruction of nature." Aristotle, in his Physics, B. iv., informs us that it was the early notion of ignorant nations that the sky was supported on the shoulders of Atlas, and that when he let go of it, it would fall.]

[Footnote 83: To a very fine purpose]—Ver. 723. "Satis pol proterve," &c. C. Lælius was said to have assisted Terence in the composition of his Plays, and in confirmation of this, the following story is told by Cornelius Nepos: "C. Lælius, happening to pass the Matronalia [a Festival on the first of March, when the husband, for once in the year, was bound to obey the wife] at his villa near Puteoli, was told that dinner was waiting, but still neglected the summons. At last, when he made his appearance, he excused himself by saying that he had been in a particular vein of composition, and quoted certain lines which occur in the Heautontimorumenos, namely, those beginning 'Satis pol proterve me Syri promissa huc induxerunt.'"]

[Footnote 84: They're asleep]—Ver. 730. "Dormiunt." This is clearly used figuratively, though Hedelin interprets it literally.]

[Footnote 85: Farm here on the right-hand side]—Ver. 732. Cooke suggests that the Poet makes Bacchis call the house of Charinus "villa," and that of Chremes "fundus" (which signifies "a farm-house," or "farm"), for the purpose of exalting the one and depreciating the other in the hearing of Syrus.]

[Footnote 86: The feast of Bacchus]—Ver. 733. This passage goes far to prove that the Dionysia here mentioned as being celebrated, were those κατ' ἀγρους, or the "rural Dionysia."]

[Footnote 87: Let's be going]—Ver. 742. Colman here remarks to the following effect: "There is some difficulty in this and the next speech in the original, and the Commentators have been puzzled to make sense of them. It seems to me that the Poet's intention is no more than this: Bacchis expresses some reluctance to act under the direction of Syrus, but is at length prevailed on, finding that he can by those means contrive to pay her the money which he has promised her."]

[Footnote 88: Rigorous law]—Ver. 796. Cicero mentions the same proverb in his work De Officiis, B. i., ch. 10, substituting the word "injuria" for "malitia." "'Extreme law, extreme injustice,' is now become a stale proverb in discourse." The same sentiment is found in the Fragments of Menander.]

[Footnote 89: Are sanctioned by custom]—Ver. 839. He inveighs, perhaps justly, against the tyranny of custom; but in selecting this occasion for doing so, he does not manifest any great affection for his newly-found daughter.]

[Footnote 90: Assistant, prompter, and director]—Ver. 875. The three terms here used are borrowed from the stage. "Adjutor" was the person who assisted the performers either by voice or gesture; "monitor" was the prompter; and "præmonstrator" was the person who in the rehearsal trained the actor in his part.]

[Footnote 91: Dolt, post, ass]—Ver. 877. There is a similar passage in the Bacchides of Plautus, l. 1087. "Whoever there are in any place whatsoever, whoever have been, and whoever shall be in time to come, fools, blockheads, idiots, dolts, sots, oafs, lubbers, I singly by far exceed them all in folly and absurd ways."]

[Footnote 92: Mould the countenances of people]—Ver. 887. He means that Syrus not only lays his plots well, but teaches the performers to put on countenances suitable to the several parts they are to act.]

[Footnote 93: Has moulded your son]—Ver. 898. "Mire finxit." He sarcastically uses the same word, "fingo," which Chremes himself employed in l. 887.]

[Footnote 94: Substance to suffice for ten days]—Ver. 909. "Familia" here means "property," as producing sustenance. Colman, however, has translated the passage: "Mine is scarce a ten-days' family."]

[Footnote 95: His she-friend rather]—Ver. 911. Menedemus speaks of "amico," a male friend, which Chremes plays upon by saying "amicae," which literally meant a she-friend, and was the usual name by which decent people called a mistress.]

[Footnote 96: And forsake you]—Ver. 924. Madame Dacier observes here, that one of the great beauties of this Scene consists in Chremes retorting on Menedemus the very advice given by himself at the beginning of the Play.]

[Footnote 97: Which he has done to me]—Ver. 954. Colman has the following Note: "The departure of Menedemus here is very abrupt, seeming to be in the midst of a conversation; and his re-entrance with Clitipho, already supposed to be apprised of what has passed between the two old gentlemen, is equally precipitate. Menage imagines that some verses are lost here. Madame Dacier strains hard to defend the Poet, and fills up the void of time by her old expedient of making the Audience wait to see Chremes walk impatiently to and fro, till a sufficient time is elapsed for Menedemus to have given Clitipho a summary account of the cause of his father's anger. The truth is, that a too strict observance of the unity of place will necessarily produce such absurdities; and there are several other instances of the like nature in Terence."]

[Footnote 98: Intrusted every thing]—Ver. 966. This is an early instance of a trusteeship and a guardianship.]

[Footnote 99: It's all over]—Ver. 974. "Ilicet," literally, "you may go away." This was the formal word with which funeral ceremonies and trials at law were concluded.]

[Footnote 100: Look out for an altar]—Ver. 975. He alludes to the practice of slaves taking refuge at altars when they had committed any fault, and then suing for pardon through a "precator" or "mediator." See the Mostellaria of Plautus, l. 1074, where Tranio takes refuge at the altar from the vengeance of his master, Theuropides.]

[Footnote 101: Amounts to the same thing]—Ver. 1010. "Quam quidem redit ad integrum eadem oratio;" meaning, "it amounts to one and the same thing," or, "it is all the same thing," whether you do or whether you don't know.]

[Footnote 102: Because my daughter has been found]—Ver. 1018. This sentence has given much trouble to the Commentators. Colman has the following just remarks upon it: "Madame Dacier, as well as all the rest of the Commentators, has stuck at these words. Most of them imagine she means to say, that the discovery of Antiphila is a plain proof that she is not barren. Madame Dacier supposes that she intimates such a proof to be easy, because Clitipho and Antiphila were extremely alike; which sense she thinks immediately confirmed by the answer of Chremes. I can not agree with any of them, and think that the whole difficulty of the passage here, as in many other places, is entirely of their own making. Sostrata could not refer to the reply of Chremes, because she could not possibly tell what it would be; but her own speech is intended as an answer to his preceding one, which she takes as a sneer on her late wonderful discovery of a daughter; imagining that he means to insinuate that she could at any time with equal ease make out the proofs of the birth of her son. The elliptical mode of expression so usual with Terence, together with the refinements of Commentators, seem to have created all the obscurity."]

[Footnote 103: By your profligacy]—Ver. 1036. It is probably this ebullition of Comic anger which is referred to by Horace, in his Art of Poetry:

"Interdum tamen et vocem Comœdia tollit,
Iratusque Chremes tumido delitigat ore:"

"Yet sometimes Comedy as well raises her voice, and enraged Chremes censures in swelling phrase."]

[Footnote 104: I don't know as to the Gods]—Ver. 1037. "Deos nescio." The Critic Lambinis, in his letter to Charles the Ninth of France, accuses Terence of impiety in this passage. Madame Dacier has, however, well observed, that the meaning is not "I care not for the Gods," but "I know not what the Gods will do."]

[Footnote 105: And close with the offer]—Ver. 1048. "Firmas." This ratification or affirmation would be made by Menedemus using the formal word "Accipio," "I accept."]

[Footnote 106: Freckled face]—Ver. 1060. Many take "sparso ore" here to mean "wide-mouthed." Lemonnier thinks that must be the meaning, as he has analyzed the other features of her countenance. There is, however, no reason why he should not speak of her complexion; and it seems, not improbably, to have the same meaning as the phrase "os lentiginosum," "a freckled face."]

Henry Thomas Riley (Translator)

Riley was born in June 1816, the only son of Henry Riley of Southwark, an ironmonger.

He was educated at Chatham House, Ramsgate, and at Charterhouse School. University was at Trinity College, Cambridge, but at the end of his first term he moved to Clare College where he was admitted on 17th December 1834 and elected a scholar on 24th January 1835.

He graduated B.A. in 1840.

Riley was called to the bar at the Inner Temple on 23rd November 1847, but early in life he worked for booksellers, editing and translating. These skills were to bring him perhaps the real jewels of his legacy with his translations of Terence, Ovid, Plautus and Lucan during the 1850's.

When the Royal Charter of April 1869 set up the Historical Manuscripts Commission he was engaged as an inspector and tasked with examining the archives of various municipal corporations, the muniments of the colleges at Oxford and Cambridge, and the documents in the registries of various bishops and chapters.

Henry Thomas Riley died at Hainault House, the Crescent, Selhurst, Croydon, on 14th April 1878, aged 61.

Terence – A Concise Bibliography

Andria (The Girl from Andros) (166 BC)
Hecyra (The Mother-in-Law) (165 BC)
Heauton Timorumenos (The Self-Tormentor) (163 BC)
Phormio (The Scheming Parasite) (161 BC)
Eunuchus (The Eunuch) (161 BC)
Adelphoe (The Brothers) (160 BC)

The first known printed edition of Terence appeared in Strasbourg in 1470.